Maternity in the Post-Apocalypse

Maternity in the Post-Apocalypse

Novelistic Re-visions of Dystopian Motherhood

Renae L. Mitchell

LEXINGTON BOOKS
Lanham • Boulder • New York • London

Published by Lexington Books
An imprint of The Rowman & Littlefield Publishing Group, Inc.
4501 Forbes Boulevard, Suite 200, Lanham, Maryland 20706
www.rowman.com

86-90 Paul Street, London EC2A 4NE

Copyright © 2022 by The Rowman & Littlefield Publishing Group, Inc.

All rights reserved. No part of this book may be reproduced in any form or by any electronic or mechanical means, including information storage and retrieval systems, without written permission from the publisher, except by a reviewer who may quote passages in a review.

British Library Cataloguing in Publication Information Available

Library of Congress Cataloging-in-Publication Data

Names: Mitchell, Renae L., 1980- author.
Title: Maternity in the post-apocalypse : novelistic re-visions of dystopian motherhood / Renae L. Mitchell.
Description: Lanham, Maryland : Lexington Books, [2021] | Includes bibliographical references and index.
Identifiers: LCCN 2021038068 (print) | LCCN 2021038069 (ebook) | ISBN 9781793605559 (cloth) | ISBN 9781793605573 (paperback) | ISBN 9781793605566 (ebook)
Subjects: LCSH: Motherhood in literature. | Speculative fiction, American—History and criticism. | Dystopias in literature. | Apocalypse in literature. | American fiction—Women authors—History and criticism. | LCGFT: Literary criticism.
Classification: LCC PS374.M547 M58 2021 (print) | LCC PS374.M547 (ebook) | DDC 813/.540935252—dc23
LC record available at https://lccn.loc.gov/2021038068
LC ebook record available at https://lccn.loc.gov/2021038069

To my long-suffering spouse, Vitaliy, who was so integral to the existence of this book.
To my daughter, Nina, whom I hope to inspire.
To Kit Hume, who gave me hope.
And to Djelal Kadir, I wouldn't be here without you, dear friend.

Contents

Introduction: Maternity in the Post-Apocalyptic Landscape   1

1   GESTATION: The Crisis of Native Pregnancy in *The Future Home of the Living God* (2017)   13

2   BIRTH: Deliverance through Plague in *The Unnamed Midwife* (2016)   41

3   NEW MOTHER: To Resist and Dis-Obeah in the Wasted Inner City of *Brown Girl in the Ring* (1999)   77

4   MATERNAL FUTURES: Maternity and the Holy Book in *Parable of the Talents* (1999) and *Who Fears Death* (2014)   109

Conclusion: Material Memory: Maternity in the Future Present   139

Afterword   143

Works Cited   145

Index   151

About the Author   153

Introduction

Maternity in the Post-Apocalyptic Landscape

At the time of the publication of this monograph, the United States and the rest of the world have undergone a series of events that the media, scholars, and its citizens have deemed apocalyptic. Primarily, the human population has been buffeted by a pandemic, the COVID-19 virus, that has caused numerous deaths and permanent injury to millions worldwide, and thus shut down or stifled so much of what we, twenty-first-century humans, consider cornerstones of civilization—education, workplaces, social centers of all kinds. Where once face coverings were considered the oppressive province of other nations, all citizenry in the United States are compelled to cover their faces to prevent infection. The year 2020 saw a record number of destructive hurricanes, wildfires, and storms in the United States, resulting in billions of dollars in damage, including twenty-two "extreme weather events" that cost over one billion dollars each. Birth rates in the United States are in drastic decline—rates that were already dropping but exasperated by the pandemic—causing researchers at the Brookings Institution to panic over the 34 percent rise of women they have determined will delay or choose not to have children in the coming years, with a continuing decline with no end in sight.[1] On the other hand, maternal mortality has been rising, and physician John Phillip Gingrey characterizes the crisis as one where

> racial and socioeconomic factors are impossible to overlook. African American, Alaska Native, and American Indian women die at a rate almost three times as high as White women. Although women of all backgrounds may be at risk, poverty is linked to the higher rates of maternal deaths. (462)

The decline in births and rise in maternal death rates—primarily among women of color—could easily emerge from a number of post-apocalyptic novels published in recent decades. It appears that the only type of apocalyptic event that has not occurred—in the past two years, especially—is an asteroid collision.

Mass events such as these drive the popularity of post-apocalyptic and dystopian fiction. Scholars of speculative fiction are aware that one apocalypse after another takes place in lived experiences around the world and in our own history, and we come to terms with these periods through displacement in future fictional settings. As scholar Daniel Drezner states in his essay on the zombie apocalypse, our interest in apocalyptic events "reflects a variety of anxieties in an American body politic buffeted by asymmetric threats and economic uncertainty" (825). The latter two events in my list above are centered in maternity, and although maternal crises do not reside at the forefront of most Americans' modern-day anxieties, the threat of a dwindling population and the subsequent threat to maternal sovereignty has likely fed into literary and film culture, as is apparent in the popularity of such television series as *The Handmaid's Tale* (2017–2021) and novels such as *Afterland* (2020) by Lauren Beukes.

The April 2017 issue of *World Literature Today* is dedicated to the prevalence of dystopian and post-apocalyptic literature in recent years, suggesting a dark future ahead—if the novelistic landscape is any indication. In her essay, featured in *WLT*, scholar Elizabeth Fifer states that "contemporary world literature's dark dystopian vision crosses cultural and geographic boundaries," pointing to a darkening horizon of eroded hope, where death is so commonplace that corpses are arranged by artists "carefully posing an intact mother and child . . . for maximum effect" (43). This scene dramatically encompasses many of the elements of dystopia that the article suggests are characteristic of these dark novels: apathy, especially regarding death; the changing role of artists when death is mundane; and the portrayal of mother and child, once a symbol of domestic tranquility now become lifeless images purposed for a shocked response—or just some response at all.

In the genre of post-apocalyptic novels, the inclusion of mother-and-child characters often serves as a post-apocalyptic trope to demonstrate the astonishing descent of human civilization: mothers and children are often enslaved or in other ways exploited, or they appear in the narrative background to illustrate the need for protection within highly patriarchal enclaves. Mothers are often posed, as Fifer's metaphor describes, for shock value or to infuse a sense of terror in a world where civilization as we know it has collapsed. In whatever dystopian setting they appear, pregnant women, mothers with infants, or mothers with children are rarely, if ever, central characters with agency in the post-apocalypse world.

However, a burgeoning number of novels of the post-apocalypse genre, which is a genre that by definition generates images of possible futures based on our choices today, portray quite a different view of maternity. These portrayals are distinctly unconventional: they propel maternal characters to the forefront of heroic prominence in the narrative. In a future devastated landscape in which human civilizations are remains left at the brink of extinction, women who embody facets of maternity—by being pregnant, a birth attendant, a mother, or in other ways maternal—are actually taking the reins of rebuilding human societies by eschewing the victimized and subject status as they are conventionally portrayed. The central argument that functions as a thread throughout this book is that perceptions of maternal characters in post-apocalyptic novels are changing from victim to protagonist, reflecting the growing view of mothers as decreasingly defined by subjection or perceived social abjection to embodying a formative role in which the maternal is a means of empowerment, self-determination, and the primary driver of the narrative. The maternal protagonists of these novels enact a significant role in the regeneration or transformation of post-catastrophe human community into one that foregrounds maternity, and reenact an analogy of civilization's rebirth that is embodied within the central role of maternal characters in this post-catastrophe renaissance.

The growing number of writers in the post-apocalypse genre who have published novels re-conceiving the notion of female protagonists as maternal figures has led to increasing attention to, acceptance of, and popularity of narrative-empowered motherhood within a genre that does not typically focus on such characters. Considering maternal characters in the post-apocalyptic or dystopian genre may bring to mind such well-known novels as Phyllis Dorothy James' 1992 novel *Children of Men*, or perhaps Marge Piercy's controversial 1976 novel *Woman on the Edge of Time*. Though these novels, among others, still evince a future post-apocalyptic landscape where maternal women display narrative agency, they often renounce the identity of mother (for whatever reason), or they exhibit maternal characteristics yet lack narrative agency, or are subjugated in a world where their fertility is a means of exploitation and is a tool wielded by male characters to gain control of the future. For example, Marge Piercy's speculative fiction is centered precisely on the topic of maternity, from its diegetic present into a future utopia. This novel is not post-apocalyptic, but speculates about the future and reflects the assumptions about maternity that underlie most post-apocalyptic novels. Yet the novel's gesture into a future speculative landscape illustrates the predicament of heroic maternity: the maternal figures who reside in the present are entirely portrayed as victims of numerous abuses, whether by physical assault or state-sponsored subjugation, which prevent these characters from playing an active role in humanity's prosperity or in the empowerment of other maternal characters. The future landscape, though, has "remedied" the apparent inescapable victimization of maternal figures. Luciente, the time-traveler from this novel's future, states that

> it was part of women's long revolution. When we were breaking all the old hierarchies. Finally there was that one thing we had to give up too, the only power we ever had, in return for no more power for anyone. The original production: the power to give birth. Cause as long as we were biologically enchained, we'd never be equal. (Piercy, 110)

The utopia described by Luciente is one that does provide an equal footing for all—allowing for the mechanization of human reproduction. However, it is precisely motherhood itself that has apparently undermined women's social parity, and thus the "conventional" maternal figures must be jettisoned as the primary cause of women's oppression. So much for maternal empowerment.

Similarly, Phyllis Dorothy James' novel centers on the "possession" of Julian, a woman who has become miraculously pregnant in a post-apocalyptic future where men are no longer able to produce viable sperm and fertility is nonexistent. Although Julian is a social activist and asserts her inclinations on where and how she wants to give birth, the male characters dismiss her assertions and instead strategize how they will use this birth to wrest the title of Warden of England from a man named Xan:

> Once he gets possession of the child his power will be immensely increased, not just in Britain, all over the world.
>
> Not his power, mine. I'm not worried about her safety . . . [I]t will be me, not Xan Lyppiatt, who presents my child to the world, and then we'll see who's Warden of England. (James, 167–168)

Even when the narrative reveals that this character, Rolf, is *not* the child's father, Julian herself is never considered as a possible contender for the title of Warden. Julian's protector, Theo, later asks Xan what he plans to do with regard to the mother of the first child born in twenty-five years:

> Xan laughed. 'I'll probably marry her. Anyway, she'll be looked after. Go back to her now. Wake her. Tell her I'm here but on my own. Reassure her. Tell her you'll be helping me to care for her. Good God, Theo, do you realise what power is in our hands?' (James, 236).

Even when Theo defeats Xan, he takes the Warden ring for himself, and the potential for leadership in this new landscape passes over the maternal character. This narrative, like the other novels on which this monograph focuses, is centered on the capability to regenerate human civilization by means of women's bodies.

However, the maternal characters in most post-apocalyptic novels that feature them are exploited, victimized, and their lives are of little value beyond their procreative ability—and they are certainly never considered for leadership roles.

My interest, in this monograph, is to critically examine recent novels that instead portray mothers, motherhood, or maternity as not only the embodied future of their narrative universe, but as principal agents that resuscitate humanity after apocalyptic collapse. The novels on which this book focuses re-conceive the notion of female characters as mothers or maternal figures as they appear in "conventional" post-apocalyptic novels that include maternal women. These characters form a resounding call back to those maternal characters that are silenced or dominated by patriarchal efforts to gain control of the future that is, potentially or perceived to be, safeguarded within the uterus. One of the most well-known recent examples of this form of domination of the maternal occurs in *The Handmaid's Tale* (1985), which points to the danger of patriarchal law run amok. Yet even in the text's frame narrative, which describes a future when forced pregnancies of the primary narrative have ended, the novel does little to empower the maternal characters, the potential mothers known as Handmaids, to fight against or gain control of the government called Gilead. In another post-catastrophe instance, Cormac McCarthy's novel *The Road* (2006) is entirely centered on a father and son relationship that has persisted despite the suicide of the protagonist's wife. She kills herself because she cannot imagine a future in which she would not be enslaved for sex and her potential to procreate. Her fears are justified as the male protagonists witness women impregnated and being lead around in chains:

> They passed two hundred feet away, the ground shuddering lightly. Tramping. Behind them came wagons drawn by slaves in harness and piled with goods of war and after that the women, perhaps a dozen in number, some of them pregnant. (78)

Another well-known post-apocalypse novel, David Brin's *The Postman* (1985), is one in which maternal characters have almost no voice at all, and when they do speak, their voices further the objectives of the male protagonists and exacerbate their own subjectivity. These are just a few of well-known and popular novels published in the past four decades that include conventional maternal characters.

Post-apocalyptic novels often implicitly ask if it is even possible, in the post-apocalyptic landscape, for a woman to maintain her independence, safety, and to take the reins of her own future when there is no longer rule of law, especially because she has presumably little protection against the bands of "wild men" who seek to possess her body and control her fertility. Yet, a number of feminist post-apocalyptic and dystopian narratives seek to challenge the premise of this assumption. This book argues that post-apocalyptic novels centered on heroic and intrepid maternal characters press upon this question by asking, instead: If maternal characters could take an active role in the regeneration of humankind after the apocalypse, what would that maternal narrative look like? This question echoes feminist scholar Judith Butler's reflection: "What would happen if 'the goods got together' and revealed the unanticipated agency of an alternative sexual economy" (*Gender Trouble*, 41)? In other words, what if maternal characters—those who assist in, or hold in themselves, the possibility of procreation—were to "get together" and resist the re-imposition of patriarchal submission and the appropriation of their agency? There are a number of questions to answer with regard to this speculative new frontier, and I believe they are finally being addressed in burgeoning maternal novels in the post-apocalypse genre.

In terms of genre, these novels are post-apocalyptic—taking place after a catastrophic event that causes a disruption of society characterized by the damage or breakdown of civilization. This genre is, in fact, a subgenre to dystopia, which focuses on a fractured civilization without, necessarily, an explicit allusion to a catastrophe that has engendered the novel's diegetic barbarism. Because these novels allude to a civilization-shattering cataclysm, an *apokalypsis*, or "unveiling" in the original Greek, I refer to them as post-apocalyptic, though I accept that some may argue they fall within the wider dystopian genre more exclusively. The narratives examined in this monograph are, more precisely, maternal post-apocalypse, a subgenre that centers on maternity and the maternal experience in the post-catastrophe universe. I will avoid placing these novels in the science fiction genre, however, although this text will make references to science fiction criticism where I deem it appropriate. The genre of dystopia, and with it, the post-apocalypse, fall within speculative fiction, a genre that lends itself to imaginative conjectures about the future.

In addition to such topics as bodily autonomy and maternal sovereignty, this monograph addresses numerous other subjects that draw important inferences from the ways that future fictional visions may re-vision maternity in our present moment. By focusing on the maternal—pregnancy, motherhood, midwifery, and so on—I am focusing on certain aspects of maternity that directly involve the presence of a uterus in the characters in the novels I examine. One of the most important concerns of the monograph is directed toward the ways in which intersectionality informs the terms and concepts this monograph leans on. I attempt to define such terms as woman, mother, and maternity with an intersectional lens, avoiding generalities and assumptions that may prove dangerous or harmful. Women do not necessarily possess a uterus, and mothers have not necessarily borne children. For this reason, this monograph sets apart maternity as centered on the uterus, whether in the arena of potential pregnancy, gestation, birth, or the postnatal period.

The examination of maternity in the post-apocalypse affords a critical opportunity to reframe maternal characters as the embodied future of human civilization and as autonomous agents who resuscitate humanity. The five novels that form the critical foci of this book each illustrate significant characteristics of the *maternal turn*, centering thematically on a stage of pregnancy and the process of becoming maternal in post-apocalyptic novels. The novels I examine are: *The Book of the Unnamed Midwife* (2014) by Meg Ellison; *Future Home of the Living God* (2017) by Louise Erdrich; *Brown Girl in the Ring* (1998) by Nalo Hopkinson; *Parable of the Talents* (1999) by Octavia Butler; and *Who Fears Death* (2014) by Nnedi Okorafor. All of these books are centered on post-apocalyptic maternity in some form, and each of them pushes back against the dystopian trope of submissive, chained, and enslaved pregnant women who have often been as much a part of the post-catastrophe novelistic landscape as collapsed buildings, burning cars, and empty highways. Taken together, these incredible novels rethink the possibilities of maternal characters in the post-apocalypse. They are not the only novels that form the new and burgeoning genre of the maternal post-apocalypse, but they are formative examples of it. The maternal post-apocalyptic genre provides preemptive lessons for the futures we wish to avoid, and for the futures in which female autonomy and maternal empowerment may be safeguarded.

Chapter 1 centers its critical lens on the novel *Future Home of the Living God* (2017), by Louise Erdrich. This novel is centered on a young pregnant woman who begins the narrative as a witness to the apocalyptic catastrophe taking place around her. The narrative follows the pregnant protagonist, Cedar, as she attempts to escape a government that seeks to imprison her and other gravid women in order to compel them to serve as "Womb Volunteers" in a period when women are giving birth to infants that exhibit the characteristics of humans at earlier stages of evolution or are simply stillborn. Cedar distances herself from her adopted mother in order to seek out her biological mother, while coming to terms with her own impending motherhood. The autocracy she flees is not a patriarchal one, but one that is identified as Mother—an all-seeing maternal government that seeks to regenerate the human population by the overturning patriarchal order and by re-conceiving the whole of society as one that is ruled by maternity.

Chapter 2 focuses on *The Book of the Unnamed Midwife* (2016) by Meg Elison. This chapter is thematically centered on the stage of parturition, which is almost nonexistent after the onset of an apocalyptic plague. The protagonist, a midwife, takes on the mission of preventing pregnancy in any surviving women she encounters, since pregnancy has become a death sentence for impregnated women. As she travels, she hears stories of and is witness to numerous stillbirths and maternal deaths, but persists in empowering the women she encounters and records these encounters in her diary. This diary forms a book that plays a significant role in the future regeneration of a new civilization, one that lauds and is centered on maternity. The narrative is surrounded by a frame story that takes place in a future long past the midwife's death, a future in which she is revered and where society is actually administered by pregnant women—upper leadership even goes so far as to wear a fake pregnancy belly as a sign of authority, and maternity is worshiped.

Chapter 3 of this book is centered on *Brown Girl in the Ring* (1998), a novel about a single mother who inherits the supernatural connection to the spirit world that is shared among the mothers in her family. However, her grandmother's ex-husband has discovered a means to "unnaturally" acquire this power, and exploits it in an attempt to gain increasing power both in the human and spirit world. He instantiates a new and repressive patriarchal structure by demanding the quiescence of the narrative's maternal characters—three generations of mothers—and the newest mother, Ti-Jeanne, confronts this scourge with her baby in tow. By ultimately embracing her maternity and her African diaspora heritage, Ti-Jeanne is able to gain the support of the deities that favor her, her mother, and her grandmother, and she fights and defeats the exploitative mob boss all while her breast-milk stains her shirt.

In chapter 4, the final chapter of the monograph examines the relationship between mothers and daughters through the novels *Parable of the Talents* (1999) and *Who Fears Death* (2014). These novels focus on post-apocalyptic communities that are formed in tandem with a particular religion and their religious texts, and these faith communities form the groundwork for new transformative post-apocalyptic cultures. In Butler's novel, a mother attempts to grow her small religious community through her writings of the religion's sacred text while searching for her kidnapped daughter. Part of the narrative is formed from the daughter's diary entries, written when she is an adult, and reflects on her mother's attempts to form a community in a post-apocalyptic milieu. Okorafor's novel takes a different angle, by following a daughter's *re-writing* of a sacred text on which the community oppression of women and mothers is based. This protagonist seeks to change the world for her mother, and for future mothers, by undermining the patriarchal prophecy of the sacred text.

INTERSECTIONALITY

Establishing the intersectional perspectives of the concepts of woman, femininity, and motherhood are critical to a text that explores the maternal. Recent decades have pointed to the evolving definition of "woman," and this evolution declared feminism's apparent death knell, but as this evolution continues, scholars have stated that

> this "apocalyptic" register demands that the feminist future be not only a forward move, but one that is produced out of the successful achievement of the political goals of the present—suggesting that we might already know in advance what feminism's future will look like. (McBean, 38)

This chronological chiasmus, one that looks forward in order to look back again, points to the importance of future-facing perspectives of maternal identity.

With the changing definition of woman, the definition of mother changes as well. But the concept of maternity remains centered on the uterus, whether in the stages of potential pregnancy, gestation, birth, or the postnatal period. Thus, maternity and maternal characters are those whose concern lies in the process of prenatal, natal, and postnatal development occurring in women's bodies (as opposed to science fiction futuristic incubators, for example), bodies that are too often severed from their sovereignty in order to exploit their procreative potential. The exploitation of maternal fertility is as much a commonplace in the present context from which speculative novels emerge as in the post-apocalyptic future, underscoring the importance of re-visions of future maternity.

Further, the emerging maternal heroic narrative also increasingly centers on mothers of color, narratives of maternal diversity that address not only the fraught deliverance of humanity from the pre- to post-catastrophe, but also press upon the complex history of women whose ethnic ancestors have undergone oppression and exploitation. The maternal diversity of the characters and contexts in these novels presses upon the complex subjectivity that women experience with regard to oppression and exploitation. Maternal characters who identify as indigenous speak to the particular context of Native maternity in North America, whose history is fraught with kidnapped infants and young children, numerous instances of rape and unwanted pregnancy, and an astonishing mortality rate among pregnant women. Other maternal characters from the African diaspora, living in North America, reach out to beliefs and cultures in diasporas related to the Caribbean and Africa to empower them within spaces that are both patriarchal and racist, overturning the social order for the betterment of all other maternal characters. What all of these novels have in common is their focus on the diverse experiences of maternity in a post-apocalyptic setting where catastrophe threatens to disempower maternal characters—a situation that speaks very much to the present day.

OVERTURNING THE PATERNAL SYMBOLIC

With the critical lens of philosopher and feminist theorist Judith Butler, among others, this book analyzes novels that employ the post-apocalyptic landscape to overturn what Butler refers to as the Symbolic. For Butler, the Symbolic (capital "S," versus the Lacanian symbolic) is

> the paternal law [that] structures all linguistic signification ... and so becomes a universal organizing principle of culture itself. ... The Symbolic structures the world by suppressing multiple meanings ... and instating univocal meanings in its place. (*Gender Trouble*, 78)

In other words, the Symbolic is centered in beliefs in repressive power structures that we often do not consider from day to day, but that affect many aspects of our lives. For example, the Symbolic undergirds assumptions our culture maintains of female dependency on the male, the unacceptability of gay relationships, the reductive idea of "tomboys" and the unacceptability of "tomgirls," the restriction of Barbies for girls and football for boys, "male-[only]" institutions such as the military, and numerous other repressive assumptions that, although sometimes challenged, are threads intricately woven into our cultural thought.

One of the most significant elements of the Symbolic in Butler's argument, and most significant for this monograph, is the element of the Symbolic centered on the Order that maintains patriarchal social structures—and is a structure the surviving male characters in these novels seek to reestablish. This Order is centered on the concept of a hegemony that forces women to choose to either actively take control of their destinies by embracing a distinctly non-maternal countenance or passively allow themselves to be reinserted into a relation of dependency due to their motherhood. The Symbolic has also driven the assumption that maternal characters simply cannot function as protagonists in the post-apocalyptic landscape. But the maternal characters of the novels on which I focus defy these suppositions by embracing maternity as either a motivation for salvaging humanity or as the means to re-appropriate control over maternal bodies by taking control of the production of future human generations. In other words, these characters employ maternity to overturn "the illusory masculine subject position" (Butler, *Gender Trouble*, 45).

These novels do not imagine a newly established matriarchy in the vein of *Herland*, but instead challenge us to see the world outside of the Symbolic by reassessing the potential of the maternal as agents of renewal in a decimated future. If we assume that apocalyptic fiction is resonant with or indicative of current political and social concerns, could it be that maternal autonomy and even *élan* serves, in part, as a response to our political climate, within which women are questioning Symbolic assumptions with regard to maternity? This is a driving question that underlies the following chapters. Each of the novels I examine focuses on distinct facets of maternity. These novels are not the first to address maternity—or its absence—as the fulcrum for the questionable survival of humankind. Examples of well-known novels such as *Brave New World* (1932), *Nineteen Eighty-Four* (1949), and the young-adult novel, *The Giver* (1993), all address questions of fertility and reproduction, but do so by entirely dominating women's potential for pregnancy. Because the post-catastrophe setting leads to a milieu in which reproduction and population growth are restricted, the novels emphasize the obsolescence of maternity rather than its potential *héroïsme*. In this way, these novels also perpetuate the Symbolic, whereas maternal post-apocalyptic novels perceive the post-catastrophe setting as an opportunity to reimagine and reframe humanity's regrowth as a means to build a maternal society from the ashes of the Symbolic.

The framework of this monograph is bolstered by a number of significant terms. The chapters utilize the terms "maternity" and "maternal" interchangeably to refer to taking part in or the general act of promoting or supporting the process of pregnancy, birth, and motherhood. However, these terms are intermittently informed and challenged by critical definitions from a number of other scholars. Julia Kristeva sees the term as one that describes either an inescapable element of humanity, or a form of erasure of identity:

> "Maternal" [is] the ambivalent principle that is bound to the species, on the one hand, and on the other stems from an identity catastrophe that causes the Name to topple over into the unnameable that one imagines as femininity, nonlanguage or body. ("Stabat Mater")

Sandra Gilbert and Susan Gubar see maternity as inextricably bound up with the womb as a cave or grave, forming the "plight of woman in patriarchal culture, the woman whose cave-shaped anatomy is her destiny" (94). Judith Butler sees the maternal in opposition within either the Symbolic or semiotic, since

> "the maternal body" designates a relation of continuity rather than a discrete subject or object of desire; indeed, it designates that *jouissance* which precedes desire and the subject/object dichotomy that desire presupposes. While the Symbolic is predicated upon the rejection of the mother, the semiotic, through rhythm, assonance, intonations, sound play, and repetition, re-presents or recovers the maternal body in poetic speech. (*Gender Trouble*, 82)

These and other controversial, contested, and generative feminist theories, among many others, will inform this book's critical analysis of the concept of maternity and emerging maternal voices in the maternal post-apocalypse.

MATERNAL POST-CATASTROPHE FUTURES

Dialogically, these novels rethink the possibilities of maternal characters in the post-apocalypse. They form a dialogic perspective that overturns assumptions of maternal capability in the post-apocalypse. They are not the only novels that form the new and burgeoning genre of the maternal post-apocalypse, but are formative examples of it. Especially in this time period when so much of the world is faced with pandemics, climate-change catastrophe, and increases in fascist-driven violence, the post-apocalyptic genre may provide preemptive lessons for the futures we wish to avoid, and for the futures in which female autonomy and maternal empowerment may serve as a regenerative course.

NOTE

1. Kearney, Melissa. "Half a million fewer children? The coming COVID baby bust." Brookings Institution, 2020.

Chapter 1

GESTATION

The Crisis of Native Pregnancy in *The Future Home of the Living God* *(2017)*

Because speculative fiction is a displaced critique of contemporary social anxieties and a commentary on social and political concerns, the genre is a vital avenue for reading into the lived experiences of writers and their milieu. However, the investigation of the political concerns surrounding pregnancy and female body autonomy is a subject that is not often explored in speculative fiction but is a significant political concern today. Reproductive autonomy is a central facet of feminist discourse and for this reason, in large part, motherhood and maternity are central topics in feminist readings of post-apocalyptic literature, and though the body of fiction confronting this issue is marginal, it is growing.

MOTHERHOOD IN PLURALITY

Critiques of post-apocalyptic fiction's portrayal of female characters are often compelled to center on the tyrannical subjugation of women's potential maternity and pregnancy, since the presence of a gravida is often accompanied by her enslavement or other forms of captivity. Yet, in recent post-apocalyptic novels that include gravid characters, motherhood is instead portrayed as a means to gain autonomy, and in some cases is even "weaponized" to regain control over women's labor in the exceptional post-apocalyptic context, challenging the typical portrayal of women's fecundity as the novelistic province of male authority.

One of the most well-known instances of the trope of the captive gravida occurs, of course, in *The Handmaid's Tale* (1985). The novel portrays an entire class of women who are subjugated for their potential for impregnation. Yet pregnancy is simultaneously the means by which the captive

"Handmaids" may achieve some hope of relief from state-sanctioned rape and abuse. The one pregnant character who receives narrative attention in the novel, Ofwarren (formerly Janine) carries the presumable child of the commander to whom she is assigned (and to whom she is subject). Janine gives birth to a child before the instantiation of the oppressive state of Gilead, but that child was taken from her upon her capture. As Ofwarren, Janine becomes pregnant, and displays this coveted *état d'être* flagrantly in order to temporarily free herself from the abuses most Handmaids suffer. Yet, her lauded maternal status is retracted when the newborn exhibits birth defects, and later dies, and she must resume her original Handmaid role. Thus, Ofwarren is at once a "former" mother, potential mother/gravida, a new mother, and subsequently returns to a state of non-mother, a situation worsened as her maternal victory is revoked and she is re-assigned to a new commander.

The consequences of "failed" maternity, however this failure manifests, are detrimental for the women of childbearing age in *The Handmaid's Tale*, who are punished with exile and are subjected to deadly manual labor. Thus, the state of pregnancy is grotesquely longed for by the Handmaids, who succumb to ritualized state-mandated rape in the hope of avoiding a potentially nightmarish existence of pain and horror as exiled radioactive waste clean-up colonists. As is often the case in highly patriarchal societies where women are harshly oppressed, subjugation is proffered as the most beneficial means of protecting and nurturing women. The commander tells the narrator, Offred, that in the pre-Gilead past, women were left to take care of themselves and their children, and as a result often had to suffer abusive and absent male partners. Now, thanks to the authoritarian Gilead, "[women] can fulfill their biological destinies in peace" (Atwood, 220). The patriarchal state operates under the assumption that a woman's fate is inevitably a maternal one, and this destiny is not one that she can choose to eschew.

The assumption of woman's inescapable maternal destiny is present in many societies even today, and with regard to the West, has only been challenged in the recent past. Teresa de Lauretis, in her book *Alice Doesn't: Feminism, Semiotics, Cinema* (1984), presses upon Sigmund Freud's theory that "the accomplishment of the aim of biology has been made to some extent independent of women's consent" (Lauretis, 131). She considers Freudian reproductive fate from a literary standpoint, and points out that even extending back into Western mythology the fecundity taking place in a woman's body was and is never entirely her own:

> The difficult journey of the female child to womanhood, in other words, leads to the fulfillment of her biological destiny, to reproduction. But the statement, objective though regretful, that reproduction is "to some extent independent of women's consent" makes us pause . . . the female child enters the liminal stage in which her transformation into woman will take place; but only if she

> successfully negotiates the crossing . . . into passivity. If she survives, her reward is motherhood. . . . Motherhood brings with it the ambiguous, negative power of Demeter. . . . Her body, like Demeter's, has become her battlefield and, paradoxically, her only weapon and possession. Yet it is not her own, for she too has come to see it as a territory staked out by heroes and monsters (each with their rights and claims); a landscape mapped by desire, and a wilderness. (131–132)

The Freudian theory of female subjection is the manifestation of a patriarchal belief that has been apparent in Western narratives since ancient times, reflected in its mythology. For example, the Greek goddess, Demeter, was raped by Poseidon, and likely Zeus as well. Her daughter is taken to the Underworld without her own consent or her mother's. This is an instance, De Lauretis argues, of a maternal body that is both weaponized and possessed, autonomously desiring and desired by male characters, operating as a Freudian biological inevitability. This premise disregards female desire by portraying her as a consumable good, subject to the whims and appraisal of the males taking possession of her body. Similarly, the literary commodification of the female body today is particularly apparent in the post-apocalyptic landscape in which human beings operate in a presumed free-for-all where the strongest males may assert dominance over women's reproductive potential, and manifest control over the destinies of these often unnamed (or renamed) women. This is the case in the feminist novel *The Handmaid's Tale*, which seeks to expose and critique contemporary threats to women's bodily autonomy but does so as women are reduced to and categorized by their reproductive potential in service of men.

The *Future Home of the Living God* (2017) by Louise Erdrich is a distinct shift from this convention, though the novel is not entirely free of patriarchal *desired* possession of the maternal body. Whereas the appearance of pregnant women in most post-apocalyptic novels has conventionally served as silent and powerless signposts for the widespread oppression of female characters, Louise Erdrich's novel portrays pregnant characters as rebellious risk-takers. Because of the fact that successful births of healthy babies are rare, the novel centers precisely on this stage of the potential of motherhood: in a post-apocalyptic world, how do pregnant women navigate the line of conventional post-apocalyptic repression and the threat of potential human extinction? The narrative centers on the pregnant Cedar, whose gravid body is sought-after by the post-apocalyptic government in a desperate attempt to control the dwindling number of successful pregnancies in the world. The attempt to take possession of women's reproductive capabilities certainly echoes *The Handmaid's Tale*, but in Erdrich's world the mothers both run and resist the increasingly fascistic direction of the government, and instead of Commanders taking control of the nation's potential pregnancies, the government takes on the identity of an authoritarian Mother who seeks to convince women that pregnancy is an ideal aspiration by seeking to befriend and identify with them. The centrality of motherhood in all aspects of power and agency is a significant turn from conventional post-apocalyptic novels, reflecting a re-visioning of motherhood in twenty-first-century culture.

The heroism of the potential mother emerges not only from the protagonist, Cedar, but from the women surrounding her who find themselves pregnant (or whom I will refer to as *gravidas*[1]). Erdrich centers her narrative on a pregnant woman who eschews the assistance and values of the male paternal figures in her life, and instead leans on the resilience of her mothers, grandmothers, and other pregnant women in order to survive and to write, despite the fact that pregnant women are "being disappeared" and even dying all around her. In spite of the novel's problematic conclusion, this chapter will illuminate the ways that a maternal perspective in the novel, as well as the mother's subversion of authoritarianism and survival through deadly childbirth, demonstrate the evolution of maternal characters in post-apocalyptic novels. Further, the imprisonment of mothers as "Womb Volunteers," which is supervised and authorized by a mysterious figure called Mother who surveils suspected impregnated women, points to a new kind of regime centered on motherhood. Thus, the presumed means of re-population of human society hinges on the command of an authoritarian Mother over the bodies of the dwindling population of potential mothers.

It is survival through the apocalyptic catastrophe that the pregnant protagonist, a *gravida*, will re-generate the human population and allow for her people, Native American Ojibwe in this instance, to reclaim the ancestral land lost to them. Although the novel ends with the gravida, Cedar, imprisoned, her body and survival will allow for the perpetuation and regeneration of the Ojibwe tribe with whom she has reunited. Numerous allusions to her connection with the Catholic figure Virgin Mary perpetuate Cedar's role as the envoy of humankind into a new state of being. Her conversations with the fetus she carries, as well as her reconnection with her Native matriarchs, point to her regenerative role. Despite the problematic conclusion of the novel, the attention that the text pays to the *process* of pregnancy and potential birth in the post-apocalypse, as well as the centrality of maternity within various forms of narrative agency, signal the critical role mothers will play in the possible regeneration of humankind.

MATERNITY IN DECLINE

The novel, divided into three parts, begins in a near and recognizable future, centered on the twenty-six-year-old pregnant Cedar. From the first sentence, the novel reveals a great deal about the background of Cedar Hawk Songmaker, which is her "white name" (Erdrich, 3). Cedar is the adopted daughter of Sera and Glen Songmaker, two "Minneapolis liberals." Cedar describes the alarming situation in which she finds herself, pregnant during a time in which human babies that survive birth are born with symptoms of "de-evolution," and upon the birth of these babies, the majority of mothers die. The novel, written in the form of a diary, is addressed to Cedar's unborn baby, referred to as "you" throughout the narrative. Cedar has decided to visit her biological family for the first time, her Ojibwe parents, seeking to learn about her genetic heritage in light of a crisis of human babies being born in earlier stages of human evolution.

Cedar has elaborate stereotypical expectations of her Native American family, but finds the reality of her new-found family disappointingly mundane: her mother, Sweetie, is married to a man named Eddy who owns a gas station, and all live together in an ordinary home on an Ojibwe reservation. Sweetie helps take care of grandmother Virginia, and also raises a daughter, Cedar's younger half-sister. Cedar finds that she initially feels very distant from the women, but she forms a quick friendship with Sweetie's bookish spouse, a man who is not her biological father. She first reveals her pregnancy to Eddy, and she shares her concerns about the apocalyptic degeneration of human beings with him. Cedar eventually reveals her condition to Virginia, then to her "BM" (biological mother), but avoids discussing the fetus' father, except when speaking to the fetus: "Your father is neither enraged nor depressed. . . . He is not a desperation junkie or a mental health survivor. He is, however, not my type" (44). Likely because of the now precarious nature of childbirth, Cedar is reticent to reveal her pregnancy to anyone, and has yet avoided telling her adoptive parents, those she is presumably closest to and who raised her.

As she travels to and from the reservation, Cedar is continuously reminded of the apocalypse taking place in the world around her, and slowly begins to realize the gravity of her changing world. She reflects on what she has heard already, she is asked about her thoughts on the situation by other characters, she follows updates in the media. In one instance, as she prepares to leave her biological mother's home, she turns on the television and hears:

> Reports are coming in of experiments hastily conducted . . . DNA experts who say on the molecular level it is like skipping around in time, and that small celled creatures and plants have been shuffling through random adaptations for months now. (44)

This frightening state of events elicits alarm in the population. Cedar then witnesses other alarming incidences: a run on her bank; her midwife disappears; and when she undergoes an ultrasound examination, the health-care workers all panic, due to the apparent surprising good health of the fetus, and must secret Cedar out of the hospital. All of these events are indications of a catastrophe underway, one that is centered on pregnancy.

Though alarm is not reflected in her narrative tone, Cedar witnesses one of the most frightening repercussions of the apocalypse: the signs of an overthrow of the government. The instantiation of repressive government is the first step toward repression of women's autonomy, and this step is clearly rendered through the suppression of the popular voice in media. According to Edward N. Luttwak's reflection on dictatorial takeover, *Coup d'État: A Practical Handbook*, "control over the mass media emanating from the political center will still be [the] most important weapon in establishing . . . authority" (131–132). The takeover of the media is a critical indication of the final steps of post-apocalyptic breakdown in all apocalyptic novels where there is still a mass media to usurp. Cedar's white father, Glen, informs her that "the government has seized the cable companies" (52). Glen has rigged an antenna in order to access any available independent media, where they see that

> the real newspeople have still not returned . . . but suddenly there is more content . . . scientists of every background pulled from the laboratories . . . as though from a dream, their faces still flattened in shock. (52)

Yet, these experts cannot explain what is happening, so the news stations have "invented a swirling set of graphics—humanoid figures growing hunched as they walked into the mists of time" (52). The "truth" as portrayed in the scientific community is one that the new regime refuses to acknowledge: that human beings are rushing toward extinction due to declines in successful maternity, and there is no known way to curtail the mysterious apocalypse.

The descent into the post-apocalyptic new world of maternal decline and oppression accelerates after Cedar has reunited with the fetus' father, who has sought her out because, he states desperately, "They're coming for you" (72). The father, Phil, reveals that Congress has voted to expand the Patriot Act to empower "the government to determine who is pregnant throughout the country . . . pregnant women will be sequestered in hospitals in order to give birth under controlled circumstances" (72). Together, they witness their first "gravid female detention" when venturing out for food. A police officer "succeeded in pulling and pushing the pregnant woman all the way up to the car. . . . A terrible sound came from the mom . . . as she was stuffed, kicking, into the [police] car" (75). This terrifying scene prompts Cedar to acknowledge her precarious situation go into hiding. Assisting gravidas into hiding is now a criminal act, though, rendering Phil an outlaw as he assists Cedar into strict concealment in her home. As the situation of unsuccessful births increases, the new laws almost inevitably expand to encompass all women of childbearing age, who are compelled to register as "Womb Volunteers" in a "female draft" to gestate embryos taken from an in-vitro clinic (90, 159, 187). With the subsequent increase in surveillance and searches, the pregnant Cedar is unsurprisingly discovered and arrested by the UPS: Unborn Protection Society.

MATERNAL AGENCY REDEFINED

Though maternity is highly valued and sought-after by the increasingly totalitarian government, pregnant women are imprisoned, abused, and dehumanized, a context that compels them to resist. Cedar is incarcerated in a hospital-like prison facility, where she shares a room with a woman named Agnes Starr. Agnes has managed to avoid being drugged, unlike Cedar, and loudly excoriates the "nurses" for the murder of gravidas, who enter delivery rooms and never leave. Agnes attempts to escape, but Cedar later finds her chained to her bed. Soon after, as Agnes is being prepared for a C-section delivery of her baby, she manages to free herself and fights her way out of the ward. Agnes is the first example of an imprisoned woman who fights her way out of the grip of the state, bringing to the forefront the author's critical view of the present-day treatment of potential mothers who in many ways are penalized For example, women in the United States are not afforded state-mandated maternity leave; are provided limited maternity care; and in the case of poor women of color, are given so little medical attention that their maternal deaths number among the highest in the developed world.[2] Agnes plans her escape and succeeds, as far as Cedar can determine, and in doing so undermines any patronizing presumption with regard to the capability of heavily pregnant women.

Cedar's next roommate is a woman of Asian descent, Tia Jackson, whom she calls the "Spider Nun," a woman who remains silent but carefully and secretly unravels blankets to construct a rope ladder in order to escape through a window. Tia remains mute and works diligently, creating for herself the opportunity to escape. At one point, during the time in which Tia and Cedar are imprisoned together, Sera infiltrates the prison and forms a plan for their escape—a mother who has found a way to rescue other mothers. Tia only begins to speak on the day of her and Cedar's escape, when she murders a nurse who finally discovers the evidence of their preparations to flee. Tia has impressively maintained the pretense of being mute in the presence of the nurse-prison guards throughout the ordeal of her imprisonment, and reveals little of her emotional state during her incarceration. But because of her deception, Tia has overheard important information: that other mothers who have given birth successfully and have remained cooperative with the government are in turn rewarded by being trained to be bounty hunters—to hunt down other suspected gravidas. This discovery reveals another stage in the maternal turn of the new despotic government—maternal women are enlisted to pursue others in a sordid form of persecution and tyranny that further closes in on women's dwindling maternal sovereignty.

Once they escape with the help of Sera—whose background as a midwife has helped her infiltrate the hospital-prison as a nurse—and by using Tia's ladder to climb through a window, they drive away in a recycling truck to a Material Recycle Facility, their new temporary home (167). This clear metaphor for the new attempt at a regenerative population increase, where conventional maternity is broken down to re-form methods of human production, is also home to the resistance that has formed against the new authoritarian regime. The recycling center is located next to a cave—an often used metaphor for both the womb and the grave stages of human existence. The degeneration of the birthing process in the post-apocalypse as a reflection of the processes taking place in the uterus echoes the words of feminist scholars Sandra Gilbert and Susan Gubar, who see maternity as entwined with the grave as a cave, embodying the "plight of woman in patriarchal culture, the woman whose cave-shaped anatomy is her destiny" (94). The metaphor is illustrated from their first arrival at the facility, where Cedar finds herself so exhausted that she observes "I have this feeling of sweetness . . . so intense that I know it must go back to my earliest days . . . before I could talk or even knew where I existed, before an I had formed into a me" (167). This embryonic description of Cedar's entrance into the recycling center is a dreamlike suffusion into maternity, but she finds the maternal space is not pleasant or safe. The decline of their situation begins just after Cedar notices a painting in a recycling bin—the painting is of a glass of water and a pomegranate, an ancient Greek reference to the myth of Persephone and Hades in the Underworld, and was known as the "fruit of the dead" (Stover, 1088). The glass of water refers to the rupture of the amniotic sac, the "waters breaking," that signals the onset of labor. Soon after Cedar has reflected on this painting—so unusual in the midst of a recycling center—Tia begins to bleed excessively and goes into premature labor. The narrative describes in gruesome detail the process of her labor and birth, and the particular difficulty of doing so in the post-apocalyptic setting. Tia must be transported through tunnels into a cave to hide from potential exposure from those who would turn the women into the autocratic authorities. These caves were emptied out due to mining, and "children have been lost in the caves, died in the caves," reinforcing the hollowed-out womb to tomb imagery and Tia's maternal journey (177). The small group travels through a "skinny, rough-walled passageway. The way gets narrower, the ceiling buckles. We hunch lower and lower until we are crawling . . . and sometimes have to inch along like a worm . . . then we come to a heavy wall with a black mouthlike aperture beneath. . . . And I . . . get stuck. Mom gently torques me this way and that . . . pulls me through inch by inch" (179). This description of the women's journey through the caverns echoes the experience of birth and the process of Tia's birthing baby by means of the capable yet stern hands of Sera. Sera assists both Tia and Cedar in a metaphorical birth into maternity, giving Cedar insight into what is to come as "we pass through a dark esophageal tunnel. 'There's a domed room, warm, just ahead,' says Mom" (180). The maternal metaphors suffuse the scene, and after several hours—and several pages—of continued agonizing labor, Tia gives birth to a still-born baby, one who "looks like any baby, a crumpled little stone-idol face.... The silence and the stillness of the baby is godly... I am on my knees. I worship" and Tia begins to croon "a song made up of sounds that I will hear later.... Sounds that were made a hundred thousand years ago" (185). The experience of giving birth to a god in the womb as a cave-grave echoes the novel's title, which refers not to Tia's womb but to Cedar's, whose fetus is "so very alive" (185). The juxtaposition of life and death, the entirety of the human experience is condensed into the cave containing a midwife, future mother, and a new unmother—to borrow a variation of Margaret Atwood's concept of the "unwoman." This compact lifetime echoes the post-apocalyptic context itself, in which many human beings are being born dead, but a few gravidas hold the possibility of new life, all taking place while their sovereignty as free human beings is under threat.

Tia subsequently escapes, with Sera's help, alongside her spouse to live as a fugitive from the "womb draft" (187). Yet Cedar remains with Sera and the resistance, traveling to the next stop as they inch toward the safety of the Ojibwe reservation. The secret resistance stronghold in the recycling center is a clear station for a maternal underground railroad, an allusion that is made clear when Cedar and Tia are first greeted: "First stop on the underground" (167). The plan is for them to stop at stations on a "truck running up north" (168). The allusions to threatened enslavement are clear. If these gravid women are captured, they will no longer be free and will be compelled to become pregnant again and give birth again and again, as long as they survive, or will be conscripted to hunt down other maternal survivors who would then descend into the same form of cyclical captivity.

The safest place Cedar can return is the reservation where her biological mother, grandmother, sister, and Eddy live. Sera and Cedar make their way to the reservation by means of a series of carefully planned routes, in disguise, and through grave difficulty. Cedar finally returns to the reservation, but the haven is not as safe as she and others had hoped, and she is kidnapped by bounty hunters and returned to incarceration. At this point, it would be logical and unsurprising for Cedar to escape imprisonment again. However, in order to underscore the apocalyptic repercussions of pregnant women who do not or cannot fight the tyrannical Mother, the author places Cedar firmly ensconced in a prison bed, functioning as a foil for the gravidas who have fought their way out of imprisonment and, presumably, remain free. Erdrich is also making a point, as Silvia Martínez-Falquina argues: "Erdrich resists the whitestream idea of dystopia, arguing instead that for Native Americans the term might refer to a realistic scenario" because indigenous people are descendants of those who survived a dystopian genocide (164). In spite of their resistance, many women of childbearing age—as was the case for numerous indigenous people in US history—fell victim to violent oppression and forced imprisonment that often lead to their deaths.

The significance of this novel among works centering on maternal post-apocalyptic heroines is centered on women's bodies and the tenuous nature of women's autonomy. The author states that the novel is very much a reflection on current political and social concerns and an entrance into the conversation on the topic of the border where a woman's sovereignty over her own *corpus* begins and where it ends. The novel weaves in Western cultural beliefs on motherhood that are literally and figuratively embodied in Marian narratives. Further, a mother as the authoritarian figurehead of surveillance is another central aspect of the narrative, which overturns the patriarchal panopticon of "Big Brother." The ubiquitous presence of Mother as she hunts down hiding pregnant women and traps them by means of their wombs for the exploitation of their wombs illustrates that a maternal post-apocalypse is not always a valorous or propitious one. Because of the complexity of these narrative elements, a close reading of the text necessitates a lens that integrates intersectional feminism in its critical reading that simultaneously presses upon the portrayal of the male characters in the maternal dystopia.

FATHERS *DEFECTUM* AND MOTHERS *INVICTUS*

The novel portrays mothers as largely taking on roles of leadership in this new world, and fathers are either absent or operating in support of mothers—an inversion of conventional parental roles in post-apocalyptic novels. The father of Cedar's unborn child, Phil, is largely absent from the narrative. Cedar makes clear that she has rejected Phil as a lover and future co-caregiver, and despite his insistent longing to be present in her life, Cedar wants little to do with him. He is briefly present during her pregnancy, however, as he persistently sought her out in a panic following the announcement of a new government mandate to arrest all pregnant women. For the subsequent weeks, Phil helps Cedar by bringing her food and other necessities, and helps keep her hidden from government agents hunting down all gravidas. Nevertheless, he ultimately ends up giving her up to authorities after being presumably tortured. When Cedar escapes from her first imprisonment, he later tries to convince her of his helplessness in her kidnapping, and insists that Cedar look on her situation in a positive light—and profit from her potentially healthy pregnancy:

> "The thing is," he says . . . "you have a treasure, Cedar, if our baby is normal. We would be in charge of things. Rich. Super rich! We'd be safe. If we somehow worked out genetically, I mean, to have a normal child the sky's the limit for us." (Erdrich, 246)

Phil has given up on resistance against the new regime and hopes, instead, to exploit Cedar's reproductive potential for privilege and freedom from oppression. However, instead of attempting to force Cedar into compliance, or capturing her in exchange for a reward, he chooses to run away without another word when Cedar calls out to her step-father, Eddy, to help her (247). The paternal figure in this relationship exhibits surprising powerlessness over his presumed dependent and helpless former lover. This confrontation between Cedar and Phil is, in fact, the last Cedar sees of her baby's father, and she subsequently relies exclusively on her mother's for help and guidance.

Erdrich's novel centers on a number of different "forms" of mother: Sera, Cedar's foster non-biological mother; Sweetie, Cedar's biological mother; Virginia, Cedar's grandmother; Mother, the new authoritarian form of government and surveillance; and the future mother paradigm, embodied in Cedar herself. In contrast to other post-apocalyptic novels in which mothers play a role, there is little domination by men over women's fertility, and almost no dependence on men and fathers for assistance despite the fugitive status gravidas and young women now embody. In fact, the figures with the most agencies in the narrative reside on the spectrum of motherhood, laid out above. Thus, the novel entirely re-imagines conventional tropes with regard to motherhood, placing maternal characters as both the central figures in human survival in the post-apocalyptic regime and as the figures of authoritative domination and oppression who seek to control the means of human survival.

SERA

Sera is the first maternal character introduced in the narrative after Cedar. She is, as is revealed early on, not Cedar's biological mother, and does not share an ethnic heritage with her adopted daughter. Instead, she is a caricature of white women who espouse the values of second-wave feminism and promotes "alternative birth practices."[3] Sera is introduced as an activist and lawyer for nonprofit groups, but is also later revealed to be a midwife. She is a vegan, anti-gun driver of a European car, and celebrates the Native American heritage of her adopted daughter to the point of fetishization. The parody of the detached privilege is embodied in Cedar's stepmother, yet she, like all of the maternal characters in Cedar's kinship circles, undermines presumptions based on her stereotypical characteristics.

Sera and Cedar do not get along, and the divide between them seems to stem, in part, from commonplace frustrations between a mother and daughter who hold different values, especially with regard to motherhood. Cedar embraces the Catholic faith whereas Sera holds secular values, and this clash comes to a head when they are finally able to discuss the pregnancy during Cedar's escape from the new state hospital-prison for gravidas. A distinct rift forms between mother and daughter when Sera expresses her displeasure with regard to her daughter's pregnancy. Cedar speaks directly to the fetus during the argument, revealing her assumptions of what it means to be a mother:

> "C'mon, just pretend you're happy," I say, my voice miserable.
> "Well, I can't. I'm hoping . . . . Well, it was very sad, but at least your friend's free now."
> . . . "Don't you dare say it!" She wants me to lose the baby. And I'm suddenly furious at my mom . . . I don't want you to be affected by her lack of instinctive love . . .
> "I know you want me to lie," [Sera] says, bitterly. "Well, tough. I can't. I wish the baby had never happened." (Erdrich, 198)

This scene reflects the distinction between Sera's unwavering practicality and Cedar's longing for a contrived and conventional motherhood that can no longer exist in her post-apocalyptic context. Cedar is angered by her mother's inability to ignore the truth, which she states is "the part of Sera I can't stand, her inability to prevaricate, to tell the nice lie, whitewash, even to make someone feel better" (198). There is a clear division here between beliefs with regard to motherhood from before the apocalyptic catastrophe and after. But it is Cedar's intransigent idealism and lack of acknowledgment of the oppression of pregnant women that in part, leads to her recapture and imprisonment at the novel's end, and Sera is all too aware that Cedar's obstinacy will lead to this conclusion.

Because Sera has rescued her daughter and hopes to keep her safe by implicitly encouraging an abortion, she becomes the most reasonable, practical voice in the diegetic new reality. Her role as a rescuer is apparent even in her name, which is not spelled as conventionally "Sarah." Instead, she is named as a seraph, an angelic being who attempts to guide Cedar to sanctuary in their new threatening and dangerous world. At the point in the novel when their argument occurs, it is clear that hiding a gravida is almost impossible, and Sera tries to make this clear to Cedar. There is some hope, due to the growing autonomy and power of the Native American reservation in which Cedar hides, that she can remain safe from arrest. But as will become apparent later on, even in the relative safety of the reservation, and even with the protective glance of the Native goddess Kateri Tekakwitha watching over her, Cedar cannot avoid being captured.

As is the case in chapter 2 of this monograph, the guardian-midwife Sera is a critical maternal character in the transitional period between the apocalyptic catastrophe and deliverance into the post-apocalyptic new world. However, in this narrative, the mother-to-be, Cedar, rejects Sera's guidance, which is a choice that leads to a devastating end for Cedar and serves as a caution for all new mothers in the future of her world—resistance against oppression must never waver.

VIRGINIA, SWEETIE, MARY, AND MARIAN SUBVERSION

The central motivation for Cedar's actions often seems to be centered on her biological mother, Mary "Sweetie" Potts. Sweetie lives with her mother, Mary Virginia, her daughter, Little Mary, and her spouse, Eddy, on the Ojibwe reservation. These three generations of women, two of whom are mothers, are a significant influence on Cedar's later decisions. The fact that they share a name with one of the most significant maternal icons of Catholicism is not a coincidence.

Cedar seeks out her biological mother in order to presumably discover possible genetic issues that may affect her fetus. However, it is clear that she actually wants to confirm what she has been told of her exceptional heritage, which is made apparent in her disappointment at the mundane reality of the Potts family business. This disappointment is exemplified in her sardonic appraisal of the biological family enterprise: "I pass the Potts Superpumper without stopping, though I do slow up a little. Well, there it is . . . my ancestral holding—a lighted canopy of red plastic over a bank of gas pumps" (14). The contrast between her expectation and reality seems to underscore a number of critiques that Erdrich is making with regard to privileged fantasies and the lived reality of indigenous peoples. This distinction is particularly important in light of the apocalyptic changes taking place around the characters in the novel.

The relationship between Cedar and her birth-mother (or "BM," as she refers to her, page 17) is a complex one, as it echoes a history of subjugation and colonization embedded in their kinship. Cedar is half-white, as Sweetie already knows, and was raised seeing her Native ethnicity as extraordinarily exotic. Cedar approaches her BM with a misplaced cultural identity, and has difficulty seeing past her fantasy of Native exceptionalism that she has cultivated while in the safety of her privileged adoptive home, and is a fantasy that is alien to—and possibly exploitative of—the reality of the Native people living on the reservation. As Cedar familiarizes herself with the reality of her Ojibwe family, her alienation gives way to a burgeoning new identity as a mother of color. Cedar begins to see herself within the maternal Ojibwe lineage, and as the bearer of one of the few healthy babies born into the diegetic present, Cedar also secures the future of the Ojibwe people in a world where modern *Homo sapiens* are being replaced by an earlier stage of human. Cedar, as a pregnant woman, will soon be hunted and driven into exile in an attempt to escape the exploitation of her childbearing body. Cedar will ultimately reject her relationship with her stepmother—the mother who raised her—in favor of her biological mother—the mother with whom she now identifies: "I've almost begun to think of her like an older sister," Cedar states, "Someone more like me than Sera, which makes me feel happy and disloyal all at the same time" (219).

The new identity that Cedar embraces, as an Ojibwe mother, is reflected in the protagonist's writings. She actively maintains a popular blog, and most of the narrative text is an epistolary directed to her future child:

> There have always been letters and diaries written in times of tumult and discovered later . . . I might be writing one of those. And even though I realize that all lexical knowledge may be useless, you'll have this record. (3)

In her writings, Cedar attempts to navigate her unique and threatened status as a "free" pregnant woman, and preserves the hope that her child "will be welcomed with eager arms into a family that spans several cultures . . . my adoptive parents . . . and you'll have aunties and uncles and a whole other set of bio-based grandparents, the Potts" (4). But coming to terms with her kinship with the Potts is a challenge that collides with the gratitude and antagonism directed toward her adoptive parents:

> My family had no special powers or connections with healing spirits or sacred animals. We weren't even poor. We were bourgeois. We owned a Superpumper. I was Mary Potts, big sister to another Mary Potts, in short, just another of many Mary Potts reaching back to the colonization of this region, many of whom now worked at the Superpumper franchise first stop before the casino. (5)

The nature of this fraught maternal legacy is reflected in narratives centered on mothers of color, particularly those who live in a form of diaspora, as Isabela Hoving states in her monograph, *In Praise of New Travelers: Reading Caribbean Migrant Women Writers* (2001): "Women writers in exile create new discourses of travel and homecoming, through which they articulate their search for new identity . . . they do find ways to express invigorating forms of bound motion" (Hoving, 75). This is likely a reflection of Erdrich's own experiences as a Native writer whose father was European and who did not live on a reservation, but visited one often (Chavkin, 55). In her novels, Erdrich often allows her protagonists to tell "stories that will let her define herself historically as a product of tribal traditions and pressures from the white community" (Reid, 78). This conflict is apparent in Cedar's attempts to come to terms with her fractured identity, as a child raised within a white and secular culture while gravitating to an indigenous, devout, alien one. Cedar seems to make choices that attempt to sever her ties from her adoptive home, despite the fact that she depends on them for her rescue. Cedar clearly wants to identify with her newfound Ojibwe family, but is constantly at a loss as to how to do so. An internal bifurcation of identities is one often faced by women of color in particular who live in cultures of historical colonialism and exploitation. In discussing mothers of color historically oppressed under colonization, Giselle Liza Anatol points out the particular challenges of women historically and narratively, whose choices and behaviors may appear counterintuitive or even self-defeating:

> The specific implications of race, cultural identity, and history must be taken into account for the reader's appropriate understanding of the family ties and gender roles portrayed in [the novel]. Throughout the Americas, women of the African diaspora must negotiate the conventional roles of daughter, wife, and mother in complex ways because they are the products of individual and historical migration patterns—both voluntary and forced. . . . [These women] are also the products of the colonial system and the ensuing anti-colonial intellectual and political movements. Colonial legacy compels many of the authors not only to challenge the notions of motherhood . . . but also to write against notions of motherhood perpetuated by the imperial "mother country" discourse and the ensuing utopian motherland ideology. (Anatol, 112)

Although centered on the African diaspora, this observation speaks to Native American women who have lived a history of displacement and colonial oppression and exploitation with regard to motherhood. The mother country, as early colonial writings make clear, is an entity to dominate and exploit, and the bodies of women of color are regarded similarly. Although the exploitation of these mothers of color has very distinct histories of oppression—the horrors of slavery versus displacement, confinement, and slaughter—they nevertheless share the challenge, as Anatol states, of the "notions of motherhood" pressed upon them. This historical exploitation is further exacerbated in the post-apocalyptic landscape, when rights for the dwindling number of child-bearing-age women are eliminated, and the notions of motherhood are equated with uterine enslavement in the form of the novel's "Womb Volunteers."

A particularly subversive characteristic of post-apocalyptic motherhood in Erdrich's novel is likely the very clear and repeated allusions to the Catholic deity and mother of Jesus, the Virgin Mary. The three generations of Mary Potts form a "second coming" of Virgin Mary, but instead of delivering human beings out of "sin," these Marys are delivering human beings through catastrophe and into the post-apocalypse. These three generations of Marys originate with the aptly named Mary Virginia, who reveals to Cedar (also named Mary at her birth) that she gave birth through "immaculate conception." Virginia tells Cedar/Mary a story of how she was engaged to marry a man named Cuthbert, but didn't realize that before she was to wed, she was already pregnant. Virginia killed a diabolical "man in blue" in her dreams, but he then appears in her waking life to cause her fiancé to die:

> "'I was visited at night in my dreams by a man in blue. . . . His instrument of pleasure, don't laugh at me, was blue also, as though dipped in beautiful ink . . .

I would lie with him all night. . . . [The] next night it would be the same again . . . I decided to kill him . . . I dreamed a knife . . . how it would fit between the dream ribs of my angel of perversion . . . "

Grandma's eyes slowly open after she's finished. . . . She tells me that she didn't know when she made those six pies for the Fat Man's Race that she was pregnant. The father of her baby was the blue man in her dream, and her son was born with strange marks. He came out with bruises on his back and bottom. So dark they looked indigo. (235–238)

Mary Virginia, true to her name, is pregnant without having physical sex, a virginal conception, a "parthenogenesis" as Sweetie states (239). Although she does marry and have eight children later on—the "old fashioned way"—her strange history nevertheless sets her apart as another Marian character, one in which "the Marian image, and characters bearing the name, appear in a variety of guises. . . . [R]eference to the Marys ('lofty' and 'lowly') . . . is that *association* of one sort or another with the Christian prototype" (De Sherbinin, 29, original emphasis). Mary Virginia names one of her daughters Mary, a woman who does not keep her child, and remains recalcitrant against traditions imposed on non-Western peoples, despite adhering to Catholicism. In this way, she redefines the Marian prototype as anti-imperial defiance in this new post-apocalyptic world, and re-envisions the new world through her embodiment of an Ojibwe (non)Virgin Mary.

The mothers of color in Erdrich's novel resist pre- and post-apocalyptic motherhood conventions in numerous ways, which highlights their roles as re-creators of the world through their autonomous reshaping of what motherhood means. The choice of how one mothers and whether or not to become a mother are aspects of this autonomous maternity. Cedar states from the early pages of the narrative that she has already had one abortion, but will carry out this pregnancy, even though it may be dangerous. She also states that she will raise the baby on her own, that the fetus' father "might help, but I'm trying to keep our distance" (6). Cedar makes it clear that she has rejected the baby's father, though she reminisces about the night when they conceived the baby. Further, she disregards the dangers of the apocalyptic events occurring around her, particularly when she disregards her adoptive parents' warnings when she chooses to seek out her biological mother, and later when she decides to live on her own. As pregnant women are being hunted, Cedar chooses to go into hiding instead of returning to either of her parents; and later when she becomes a fugitive, she pushes against pressures to abort her pregnancy. Whether or not her decisions are "practical" or rational, she often chooses to push against pressures from non-Native characters, including her stepmother and her ex-lover, Phil, the baby's father, paving her own way alongside her biological mothers in the new post-apocalyptic reality.

Cedar's personality echoes that of her biological mother, who both embraces Catholicism and is staunchly independent, seeking the acceptance and advice of no one else. Sweetie is a mother of color resisting colonial values and ideology in spite of her embrace of a colonial religion. Early French colonists of the area in what is now Minnesota brought Catholicism with them, and this religion was imposed on the indigenous population, including the Ojibwe. Yet Sweetie, who reveals in her first phone conversation with Cedar that she is Catholic, advocates not for a Virgin Mary but a Native goddess-saint statue to be erected on the reservation (13). As she later presents her proposal for a shrine and the erection of the statue to the tribal council, someone points out her apparent religious contradiction, characterizing her supposed idolatrous frenzy as "traditional religion," rebuking her for promoting a pre-Christian belief system. Sweetie dismisses the critique unequivocally, and seeing no need to defend her proposal, simply states "I'm a pagan Catholic. Moving on?" (23). Sweetie continues by arguing for the financial benefits of instantiating a pilgrimage site, especially in this apocalyptic moment, further underscoring her defiance of "acceptable" religious piety by looking to the possible profit the statue could bring. The intersection of economic, "pagan," and imperial beliefs converge at the soon-to-be constructed pilgrimage site, which is where the narrative catastrophe reaches its pinnacle, as this is the very location where Cedar will be later kidnapped and taken to be re-incarcerated. Cedar's story is similar to historical figure of Kateri Tekakwitha, as the saint was also kidnapped and, like Cedar, refused to marry a man despite social pressures to do so. As Cedar helps Sweetie with preparing the ground for the shrine, Cedar observes: "My new mom and I are left with the hose, watering down the grass. This is how the world ends, I think, everything crazy yet people doing normal things" (25). But, of course, what the two women are doing is not normal: constructing a pilgrimage site of Sweetie's devising, which is erected without the typical sanction or blessing of the Catholic Church but through the efforts of mothers and will become a significant post-apocalyptic locus for the indigenous community.

Sweetie is, further, an unconventional mother. During her fugitive stop at the reservation, Cedar has a conversation with Sweetie away from the other mothers who are sitting in the house, worriedly strategizing Cedar's escape. She smokes her cigarette near the pregnant Cedar, and asks "What do moms and daughters talk about?" (219). The conversation moves to Cedar's own birth, and Sweetie describes herself as a pregnant "punk": "Imagine. Me at nine months and neon-yellow mohawk. Rings and studs everywhere possible .... The delivery nurses kept coming in to take our picture" (220). Sweetie shows Cedar one of the photographs portraying a young Sweetie covered in piercings, and Sweetie admits, "Yeah, pretty weird I guess" (220). Sweetie reveals that she had had an affair with Glen, whom Cedar discovers is not her adoptive father but is, in fact, her white biological father. Sweetie's affair with a white man is another further shocking irreverence, but she will not be restrained by rules or conventions. When she later takes Cedar to pray to at the feet of the statue of Kateri, Cedar is detected by drones and is later kidnapped by the Mother government.

Cedar unwittingly follows in the footsteps of the two generations of mothers before her. Cedar states that her Native ethnicity made her exceptional, in the eyes of her stepparents:

> My ethnicity was celebrated in the sheltered enclave of my adoptive Songmaker family. Native girl! Indian Princess! . . . [E]ven as a theoretical Native . . . I always felt special . . . I supposedly had a hotline to nature. (4–5)

Cedar is inherently an outgrowth of the earth, chthonic, and "rare, maybe part wild" (4). As an apparent extension of Mother Earth, she is inherently maternal, and her identity is rooted in fecundity. In some ways, this contrived connection with the earth is a way to, perhaps, poke fun at the exoticization of Native people among privileged white people, whose adoption of Native American names and concepts for sports teams and nature camps, appropriation of rituals such as drum circles, "smudging" as a means cleanse a space, adoption of "spirit animals"—all despite the continued oppression of Native peoples on whose land they reside. But Cedar's name also seems to point to her role as an *axis mundi*, as the novel's title suggests—Cedar carries a rare healthy baby that makes her central to the re-empowerment of the Ojibwe. Thus, *she* is a gestational home for a future "living god"—a chance for the survival of modern humankind. However, as a manifestation of "Mother Nature," Cedar is subject to domination in what Anatol refers to as the "intersection of geography and gender ideology" (112). Feminization of landscapes is a common colonial trope, as Anatol explains: "Explorers' discourses feminized landscapes and visualized them specifically in terms of heterosexual fertility, their feminine and maternal metaphors lacked any accompanying associations of authority and nurturance" (112). Thus, the association between Cedar and imperial feminization of land is a form of exploitative ideology that Cedar is resisting.

MOTHER IS THE NEW AUTHORITARIAN IN TOWN

The post-apocalyptic worlds that appear in utopian or dystopian novels seem to have one thing in common: when a form of government emerges after the apocalyptic catastrophe, that government is nearly always authoritarian. Maria Manuel Lisboa observes, in her 2011 book *The End of the World*, that

in numerous narratives, ranging from canonic texts to popular science fiction
... following the advent of large-scale catastrophes and ensuing social collapse, autocratic regimes almost invariably assume control. In many post-apocalyptic dystopias ... we find strong hints that after global events of a cataclysmic nature, authoritarian statuses quo tend to emerge as the default social organization. Furthermore, these new autocracies, and the brands of alienation they sustain, may turn out to be quantitatively but not qualitatively different from social structures ostensibly supposed to be or to have been essentially democratic. (91)

The critical tendency of post-apocalyptic literature, as is true among other genres of speculative and science fiction, reflects the often problematic democracy of today, as Lisboa states. But the criticism is pointed toward the authoritarian—or even fascistic—tendencies of these social structures: the restriction of women's corporeal autonomy, the oppression of nonbinary sexual relationships, the explicit and implicit abuses of minority races and ethnicities, and so on. These forms of oppression are characteristic of authoritarian regimes, and yet characterize Western democracies today. Though a superficial tolerance for diversity remains, numerous minority groups continue to appeal for fairness in a justice system and culture that occasionally awards them degrees of equity, and perpetually threatens to take it away again.

Erdrich's novel falls within the scope of a fictional criticism of Western democratic ideology, but the significant distinction between the novel's autocracy and those of other post-apocalyptic novels is the fact that this one identifies as not as the patriarchy, fatherland, or father figurehead, but rather as Mother. This unusual form of autocracy, centered on a *maternal* despot, undermines conventions of post-apocalyptic autocracy. The Orwellian Big Brother face of totalitarianism has been supplanted by an insidious Big Mother. Despite the fact that pregnant women all around her are being captured, Cedar's first encounter with Mother is through her computer. The encounter first occurs as Cedar is writing a new entry for her successful blog, which is based on her experiences and thoughts through a Catholic lens. She is writing down her thoughts on what the Virgin Mary's experience of pregnancy must have been like when she abruptly breaks down weeping, imagining that the being growing in her uterus may not be human. Suddenly, though she has not touched her computer, a woman's face appears on the screen: "'Hello,' she says, just to me, her eyes meeting mine. 'I am Mother. How are you today?'" (68). Cedar remembers that her camera is taped over, and despite the fact that she presses the power button, the computer does not turn off.

Mother continues to ask Cedar how she is doing, her voice "drenched in warmth." The novel describes her matronly face: "Her face is round and white like pizza dough. Her cheeks sag. Her smile is tiny with stripes of red lip. Her brown hair, a Prince Valiant helmet, sits firmly on her skull. Her shrewd brown eyes twinkle" (68). The uncanny combination of her sudden appearance, her egregiously average middle-aged visage, and inescapable eye contact with Cedar is horrifying, and the fact that Cedar can't seem to wrest control of her laptop from Mother seems to allude to an Orwellian Big Brother who watches without warning or consent. The feigned concern adds to the terror, and thereafter Cedar "avoided the computer after it conjured up the helmet-haired entity" (69). Cedar begins to panic, and avoids using her cellular data, location services, and checks the news only once a day. Although she does not say so explicitly, Cedar knows she is being tracked somehow.

After some time passes, Cedar decides to work on her church's newsletter, which she can edit through her computer's word processor without any connection to the outside world. Nevertheless, as she is writing offline, Cedar's

> screen goes dark and swirly. This time she floats slowly into focus from the depths. "Hello, dear. How are you?" Her full cheeks are cement gray this time, set hard around her smile. "Mother is thinking all about you. Would you like to tell me about your day?" (71)

Cedar shuts down her computer, and at the same time her former lover, Phil, arrives at her door, to warn her that pregnant women are being rounded up:

> The House and Senate have voted to strengthen and give new powers to . . . the Patriot Act . . . which still allows our government to seize entire library and medical databases . . . [and] empowers the government to determine who is pregnant throughout the country . . . pregnant women will be sequestered in hospitals in order to give birth under controlled circumstances. (72)

With this authoritarian turn, Cedar has now become a fugitive, but she realizes she has few places to hide. When discussing the COVID-19 virus and other pandemics, Slavoj Žižek describes in his book on the new post-apocalyptic reality, *Pandemic! 2: Chronicles of a time Lost* (2020), a growing form of "surveillance capitalism," where "a new phase of capitalism wherein total digital control is exerted over our existence by state agencies and private corporations" (13). This form of surveillance, which permeates nearly all forms of communication, is apparent in Cedar's context by limiting her ability to communicate freely, controls her actions and choices.

The emergence of Mother is distinctly different from other appearances of such Orwellian characters as Big Brother, since her demeanor portrays an apparent friendship and empathy, hoping to gain the trust of the user she is surveilling rather than forcing compliance with fear and intimidation. The sudden appearance of Mother is not one the reader would find particularly shocking—we all assume that our use of the internet and social media leaves us vulnerable to surveillance, and we assume that our data is being collected by large media companies and possibly by government agencies as well, since "the extensive use of surveillance has been quietly accepted in many parts of the world" (Žižek, 13). But Mother's direct address of Cedar, the manifestation of her facade without warning—even when the computer is offline, and her appeals to Cedar's well-being are all uncanny and even terrifying. Clearly, also, the mock-friendliness of the matronly apparition is meant to instill a sense of the inescapable power of Mother, who knows where you are and has captured you.

The fact that Phil warns Cedar of the expansion of the Patriot Act immediately after this episode with Mother is significant, and points to our present-day surveillance state where such a Mother figure is not a far-fetched concept. The Patriot Act, instantiated in 2001, allowed for the collection of data of millions of Americans, largely based on phone records. In this vein, under the Foreign Intelligence Surveillance Act (FISA), an amendment was passed in 2008 under which the FBI created the PRISM program: the code name for a National Security Agency (NSA) program allowing for the collection of internet communications requiring only "court-approved search terms." In May 2020, the US Congress voted on whether or not to pass an amendment to the Patriot Act to specifically restrict internet browsing and internet search histories from what the government is allowed to collect through the approval of any secret court. The passage of this amendment failed by one vote. Thus far, then, there seem to be few if any checks on the government's ability to infiltrate and surveil internet activity by unindicted civilians. The continued expansion of powers of the government to collect civilian and consumer information can easily lead to the detention of whatever group authorities seek to detain—even pregnant women. Cedar has used old and untraceable insurance cards during her doctor visits, and has taken other measures to conceal her whereabouts. But Cedar realizes, though, the way in which she has given herself away, when

> in the middle of the night, I sit up, eyes wide. I used my credit card to buy baby clothes . . . I paid my credit card bill online . . . I am being pregnancy-purchase-tracked by Mother . . . we are already half-way found. (73)

With the government's ability to collect what was once private information, pregnant women need only slip up once in their online activity and they can be tracked and discovered by Mother. Cedar and Phil decide to bury their cell phones in a graveyard, since location tracking cannot be turned off anymore, and though sometimes "the internet works . . . I've told Phil how this Mother apparition appears and he agrees we can't use it" (81). But it is already too late.

Cedar seeks out her adoptive parents for help, but they have disappeared. One day, when she calls their landline home phone, a new voice answers:

> A woman says, "Songmaker residence, can I help you?" The overly pleasant voice is not my mom's, but it is familiar. Fulsome, full of inquiry, too avid. . . .
> All day, I keep hearing that voice, the lilt increasingly sinister, *Can I help you?* A parodic melody. *Can I help you?* (73, original emphasis)

The government Mother has infiltrated Cedar's parents' home. Sera must suspect that Cedar is trying to contact her, so she leaves a note under the door: "Don't call us, honey, and don't leave any messages. We're all right. Stay safe. We took all of the records" (76). The narrative is unclear whether or not Sera knows about Cedar's pregnancy, but it is clear that Sera is aware that Cedar is being pursued by the new regime. Cedar grows to understand where Sera has gone: like the protagonist of Meg Elison's *The Book of the Unnamed Midwife* (2014), Sera has joined the "underground midwives" and hopes to assist in the delivery of babies in resistance to the authoritarian Mother (108).

At one point, it is clear that civilization is rapidly collapsing, and there are food and gasoline shortages. Phil has access to some remaining resources in the basement of a church where he and Cedar first met. He brings home a television that works intermittently, and one morning, when they turn it on, they

> see the image of Mother fading in and out. She looks haggard, much older, tinged with green like the head of the Wizard of Oz. "I am back," she says, glaring exhaustedly up from under her eyebrows. "They failed to destroy Mother. I will always be here for you . . . I wonder if you have the courage to save the country we love. We need you to be a Patriot. We need you to volunteer. If you are a woman, if you are pregnant, go to any of our Future Home Reception Centers." (90)

The demand to succumb to the State appeals to a nationalistic ideology: true "patriots" will cede their freedom for the betterment of the whole—whether that whole includes other citizens or the capitalist need for a future supply of labor.

The hunt for gravidas has expanded to all non-gravid women of childbearing age to submit to attempted impregnation, Cedar realizes: "Someone describes a raid on an in-vitro clinic by members of some militant organization. . . . They plan to use one thousand Womb Volunteers to gestate the embryos they've liberated from that clinic's deep freeze" (90). The narrative implies that there has been a reprisal against Mother, but the regime has prevailed and maintains control, expanding its search for any women who can possibly gestate future babies. The nationalistic language to compel submission to the regime is driven by Mother, who appeals to women's "patriotism" to submit their bodies to the WV centers in an attempt to repopulate the country.

There is a racist component to this new stage of oppression, with regard to the embryos that have been taken. Mother states: "We took the leftovers. The embryos not labeled Caucasian. We're going to have them all and keep them all. We're not killing any. All are sacred" (90). The value of human life has changed in a society that has historically treated citizens differently based on race differences, but the distinction remains: embryos of color are nonetheless "leftovers" while simultaneously "sacred." As stated in the text *Critical Race Theory*, "only those who were deemed white were worthy of entry into our community," and others, of course, are seen as "less than," becoming sacred when the laboring population is threatened with extinction (Delgado, 87).

Being disregarded as "less than" actually provides an outlet for the Ojibwe characters in the novel. In a letter to Cedar, Eddy writes,

> Our tribe has formed a militia quartered at the casino. Quite a number of us see the governmental collapse as a way to make our move and take back the land. Right now, nobody gives a rat's ass what we do. (95)

For this reason, he urges Cedar to find a way to escape to the safe haven of the reservation, which has become increasingly autonomous. The urgency increases when Eddy finds a way to visit Cedar in person, where he discusses a plan for escape, and as he is leaving. While he is there, Mother appears:

> My computer switches on. All by itself. . . . Nobody has touched it. We whirl to it in surprise. It isn't plugged in and I have let the battery die. "Hello dear, this is Mother. How are you tonight? I am worried. We don't seem to be communicating very well." Phil steps behind the computer, jerks it up, and smashes it on the tile counter. But it won't disintegrate. "Please get in touch with Mother. Please get in touch," it says, in pieces on the floor. (119)

The technological ability of the new regime is increasing, and the technology is centered on finding Cedar.

Cedar and Phil have chosen not to leave with Eddy, and soon after Cedar is captured. One of Mother's agents, who is a physical avatar of the digital Mother, arrives at Cedar's home. This woman, who has dark skin, picks the lock of Cedar's house and

> poked her head around [the door] with a cheery halloo! was round and honey-brown, all sorts of pretty, a mixture of several races. Her face was delicately freckled and her straightened auburn hair . . . sprayed away from her forehead and cheeks in a Betty Crocker halo. She wore jeans, Keds, and a raspberry cotton tunic sweater . . . she carried a covered basket . . . [that] held a handgun beneath the red and white checkered napkin. (123)

This exaggerated matronly archetype of Mother is unlike other government agents in post-apocalyptic narratives. Unlike the typical male and flagrantly armed police force of other novels such as agents of The Eyes in *The Handmaid's Tale*, these women use another weapon to mollify their captives: as Cedar admits, "I have this weakness. Nice people paralyze me. Dark skinned people who are nice, especially" (123). This "niceness," the motherliness that characterizes Mother, is precisely the weapon that these agents count on to bring in their "Womb Volunteers" undamaged. She transports Cedar not in a police vehicle but in a mundane silver Camry, and Cedar later learns that the agent is a former US Marine who now works for the Unborn Protection Society (UPS). This image entirely undermines the conventional concept of the post-apocalyptic secret police force, and demonstrates the once-unthinkable idea that an authoritarian regime can be run by a mother who identifies herself as such, deploys mothers as her agents in order to capture future mothers for the good of the Mother autocracy.

Cedar is taken to a detention center for gravidas from which she later escapes with Sera's help. After numerous ordeals, they finally reach the Ojibwe reservation, and Sera and Cedar discuss their situation, including the fact that the air is now filled with insect-sized drones and "listeners" that are no larger than specks of dust. Because of the infiltration of Mother through consumer technology, nearly everyone is discarding their devices: "There are piles of them in the landfills and reclamation centers, all smashed and waterlogged. . . . Sweetie's fired up the vintage radio. . . . Vintage is the new *au courant*" (223). Incredibly, like the babies that are being born in earlier stages of human evolution, technology is also moving backward in the post-apocalypse. Alongside the use of old radios, there are runners—town criers—who deliver the news to different sites around the reservation. But the technology utilized by Mother is highly advanced, and inescapable, as Cedar notices: "something flickers around me, a tiny bird, clicking and whirring. And a transparent oval floats past my clasped fingers . . . I've been seen" (231). Soon after, while Cedar is sleeping in Little Mary's room, Cedar is awakened by a small sound and dogs barking. Hiding in the midst of Little Mary's clothing and detritus, Cedar sees a woman walk in who looks straight at her:

> It is Mother. Her thick hair is fiercely sprayed, the bangs immobilized. Her dark eyes are sunken in her dough face. Her lipless mouth puckers in sympathetic consternation. "Are you in there, dear?" . . . I realize that Mother can't even see me beneath all of these wads of clothing. . . . Mother looks like she's already been shot. As she takes in the overpowering chaos and layers of developed filth, her mouth opens and shuts. . . . With an air of sacred awe, Mother backs out of the room. (240)

Although Mother has tracked Cedar to this place, the gravida is temporarily saved by the unbelievable and unexpected disorder of Little Mary's room. However, Phil appears soon after, drags her out of the room, and explains that Mother will return with reinforcements. He helps her hide out in Eddy's gas station, and confesses to being held by Mother's agents until he could escape. He learned that "it's a global crisis, it's the future of humanity, so you can see why they need to keep an eye on women. Every living thing is changing, Cedar, it's biological chaos" (246). Cedar's eventual capture, and the seizing of her baby, is inevitable. But Phil makes her an offer: if they voluntarily turn in the baby together, then they can be rich and "in charge of things." Cedar rejects him, and he escapes, but his implicit warning turns out to be true. Soon afterward, while praying to the statue of Saint Kateri, Cedar is taken.

Cedar is taken to a correctional facility that has been transformed into a birthing center. While there, she is subjected to "mandatory Watching Hour," which is a form of re-education similar to the "Two Minutes Hate" that was daily mandatory viewing in George Orwell's *1984* (1949). In this form of brainwashing, "Mother is the only channel.... Mother surges into view, round cake-pan face, busy calm" (254). During the Watching Hour, Mother repeats incessantly that the fetus each of the women carries is a "divinely infused eternal soul" and "you can be absolved of anything you did ... by contributing to the future of humanity. Your happy sentence is only nine months" (254–255). As the indoctrination continues, Cedar realizes "We are not allowed to look away" (255). The indoctrination is so thorough that as Cedar is taken for an ultrasound and examination, she must make a significant effort so she can "block out Mother's voice," though it's a voice she can no longer hear (256).

The authoritarian figure undergirding the post-apocalyptic tyrannical state of Erdrich's novel is a reflection of our present-day surveillance state and a caution for the future. The stage has been set for an autocratic takeover. If a crisis such as the one depicted here—or in *The Handmaid's Tale*, or other post-apocalyptic novels, for that matter—were to take place, these novels ask, are we able to defend against a regime that knows about our histories and proclivities better than we can remember them ourselves?

AMNIOTIC TRANSITION INTO THE POST-APOCALYPSE

Christina Tourino states in a 2003 article that

> the amniotic is ... crucial to ... extended meditation about ethnic mothering in desperate circumstances ... the amniotic space [is] the source of the unvoiced ethnic story, but also ... a site of ethnic reproduction contested by the ... government. (134)

This anxiety, an anxiety perpetuated by governmental forces with regard to unacceptable nonwhite mothering, is central to Erdrich's novel, which is scaffolded by the protagonist's conversations with her silent but often agitated fetus. In the intra-catastrophe period, as the world transitions into its post-catastrophe state, Erdrich's novel illustrates that it is the pregnant woman, particularly the pregnant woman of color, who must concentrate her energies on mere survival as the means to deliver her child and a new generation of humanity into the post-apocalypse. Mere survival of the ethnic gravida is one of the most significant means by which the maternal protagonist adopts the mantle of heroine in her world, one in which the controlling regime is determined to colonize or exterminate her people on both sides of the apocalypse.

Through the protagonist's journal reflections, the narrative continuously draws a distinction between those who are white and those who are not. The narrative focuses on female characters who perform motherhood and identify as mothers and these women, white and nonwhite maternal characters, are the individuals who possess the power of rebuilding society, yet are at odds as to who will maintain control and survive as a deadly devolution takes hold over the present generation of infants. The central characters in this conflict, other than Cedar, include Cedar's Asian cellmate, Tia; Cedar's adoptive mother Sera; her biological mother, Sweetie; and the pervasive white Mother, who performs surveillance and mysteriously controls communicative technology throughout the novel. Although the fathers play ancillary roles as accomplice rescuers, the primary possessors of narrative and regenerative power are the maternal characters.

ESCHATOLOGICAL INDIGENEITY

Cedar is a liminal character in numerous ways: she is Ojibwe and white; she is in a gestational state, between non-mother and mother; and she stands at the limin of human existence. For most of her life, the protagonist identifies with her Native American heritage, and although she refers to herself as a "theoretical Native," she embraces her family's efforts to recapture land that was taken from them through colonial theft, and she accepts what she sees as her role within her maternal Ojibwe heritage. Raised by an upper-class white couple who treat her as exceptional, Cedar has never experienced the struggles of most indigenous people, but she is open to education about this unknown half of her family. Erdrich makes Cedar's maternal role clear; she is a Marian character whose child will be a savior for the Ojibwe people, at a time when her people can take back their land and possibly perpetuate their heritage: she is a third-generation Mary Potts, born to a woman named Mary Potts, who is daughter to a Mary Potts. This new identity does not come easily to Cedar/Mary, because she must break through her privilege and the stereotypes she has unknowingly embraced, which all come to the forefront when she first meets her Native mother:

> Who are they to have destroyed the romantic imaginary Native parents I've invented from earliest childhood . . . who died in some suitably spiritual Native way—perhaps . . . carried off by thunderbirds? . . . I wouldn't have had the slightest thing to do with them if it wasn't for my baby. (6)

Indeed, the protagonist employs this pregnancy as the impetus to rewrite her life, in a literal and figurative sense, and the novel is the result of this composition.

The largely epistolary novel begins with Cedar's brief reflections on the first four months of her pregnancy and the events leading her to reconnect with her Native biological family. In order to pave the route for the future "living god," as the title suggests, Cedar must learn how to deliver her baby as an Ojibwe, which will require a process of self-discovery, as she explains to her fetus:

> I think you need to enter the web of connections that I never really had . . . which also means that I've got roughly four and a half months to figure out how to give you a coherent family as well as be a mom. (6)

The novel covers precisely these four-and-a-half months, during which the narrator contends with the country's governmental collapse and the new ruling regime that, due to the mysterious de-evolution that is occurring in all newborn babies, endangers her plans to raise an Ojibwe child by threatening to take away her child and her freedom. The laws are not quite in full effect in the first weeks of the narrative, but Cedar mentions a law that *has*, in a sense, been in effect for quite some time, through the Indian Child Welfare Act. This law, she states, "makes it almost impossible to adopt a Native child into a non-Native family," and she fears that this, among other authoritarian rules, may justify the taking of her child (4). The United States has a long history of forced removal of Native children from their tribal groups and from their families, which historically threatened the survival of Native nations. Beginning in the late-nineteenth century, the United States implemented its "Boarding School Era" of forced abduction and assimilation of Indian-American children. This abduction and assimilation continued even after the last boarding school shut its doors, by means of the foster and adoption system, which took Native children from their tribal groups and relocated them into white families. This treatment of Native children slowed only when the Indian Child Welfare Act was implemented, although this law did not eradicate these forced relocations entirely, and later justified other abuses of indigenous children.

Erdrich's novel underscores the inhumane treatment of Native families through the new colonization of pregnant bodies. The post-apocalyptic landscape is a fitting context through which Erdrich can draw attention to the long history of forced removal of children. The horror of these removals is reflected in the narrative, through laws enacted on pregnant and later all childbearing-age women compelling women to become "womb volunteers," or essential incubators for babies that will be taken from them upon birth. This law, extreme in its universal treatment of women of *all* ethnic backgrounds, seems possible because of the groundwork set by the historical treatment of Native women, and women of color. Cultural extermination by means of stolen progeny is one of the most insidious and destructive means by which the US government is known to have treated Natives in the country's early history. Tourino's exploration of "ethnic mothering" through the "amniotic space" in the work of writer Joy Kogawa is resonant with the plight of Native family survival, and articulates the precedent that threatens all women:

> By connecting Naomi's family to Natives, Kogawa frames Japanese-Canadian suffering with the much older tragic history of Native American extirpation by whites. Once a sovereign nation, the Natives have become little more than a commodity fetish. (141)

The destruction of Native sovereignty is apocalyptic, and the threat to female sovereignty is equally so. The precariousness of sovereignty is central to the novel, not just in the contested sovereignty of women's bodies, but also in the reclamation of national sovereignty that takes place in Mary Pott's Ojibwe reservation. In this way, the narrative draws a parallel between the attempted extermination of Natives' and women's autonomy, both of which are centered on the fulcrum of amniotic space. Therefore, the tragic ending of the novel is a necessary one in underscoring the pain and imprisonment that indigenous women have suffered throughout the history of the United States.

This novel is not the first to address the amniotic space as the fulcrum for the questionable survival of humankind. Well-known novels such as *Brave New World* (1931); *Nineteen Eighty-Four* (1949); and the young-adult novel, *The Giver* (1993) are highly lauded novels that all address the question of fertility and reproduction in the post-apocalypse. However, these narratives are centered on the means of exerting control over women's potential for pregnancy. Population growth is restricted, and the novels emphasize the obsolescence of maternity rather than its intrepidity. In Erdrich's novel, the protagonist slowly reaches the realization that she is no longer a sovereign being with the freedom to move about freely not because her pregnancy is interdicted, but because her fetus is highly coveted by the new government, embodied by Mother. Thus, this unusual example of maternal apocalypse features maternal heroines and victims, autocrats and antagonists, all pointing to a post-apocalyptic world that is altogether maternal.

NOTES

1. "Gravida" is a term in human medicine that refers to a pregnant woman, and though the term may seem cumbersome, it is quite useful for this monograph's purpose.

2. For example, the U.S. Department of Health and Human Services concluded in a National Vital Statistics Report (January 2020) that black women died 2½ times more often than white women during or after birth ("Evaluation of the Pregnancy Status Checkbox on the Identification of Maternal Deaths").

3. The values of second-wave feminism birthing practices are evinced in such texts as *Our Bodies Ourselves* (first published in 1970). Although the movement promoted the goal of moving away from the medical establishment with regard to obstetrics, this goal largely welcomed only white, upper-middle-class women—such as Sera.

Chapter 2

BIRTH

Deliverance through Plague in
The Unnamed Midwife (2016)

> *So God was kind to the midwives and the people increased and became even more numerous. And because the midwives feared God, he gave them families of their own.*
> —Exodus 1: 20-21,
> New Oxford Annotated Bible

Meg Elison's novel, *The Book of the Unnamed Midwife* (2016), earned numerous awards following its publication, including the prestigious Philip K. Dick Award as a distinguished and original science fiction novel. The novel closely examines circumstances similar to those in the post-apocalyptic scene above, in which conventional family structures are changing due to the concern over women's ability and opportunity to bear children. Yet this novel reframes the post-apocalyptic preoccupation over women's fertility and sovereignty, and the distinction between Elison's novel and novels such as David Brin's highlights the maternal turn in post-apocalyptic protagonists. There are numerous issues at play in this scene, above, from the 1985 novel *The Postman*: the danger of infertility, the centrality of the "father's body" and "non-men," and the preservation of pre-apocalypse marriage arrangements in a world of diminishing population. These concerns are apparent in such scenes as the following, where patriarchal values regarding marriage and appropriate sexual conduct continue to dictate with whom women may have sex, but men are not held to this restriction and may instead act as an anonymous inseminator if they choose:

> "And then Mrs. Howlett thought you'd be perfect for helping me and Michael finally have a baby . . ."
> Gordon blinked. "Um," he said . . .

Abby went on quickly. "Well, it would cause problems if we asked any of the other men here to . . . to be the body of the father. I mean, when you live close to people, like this, you have to look on the men who aren't your husbands as not being really 'men' . . . at least not that way . . . it might cause trouble." (Brin, 61)

Elison's novel takes these concerns, which are commonplace in a number of post-apocalyptic novels, and places them in a setting that strains the possibility of perpetuating pre-apocalyptic ideologies. Elison revisions the world in which human populations are decimated, and presents a landscape in which potential mothers are unable to neither survive childbirth nor carry out live births. This precarious condition leads to a new sovereignty for the few surviving women, a sovereignty that is instantiated by eradicating the debris of what Judith Butler refers to as the Symbolic—a systemic social framework that is driven by patriarchal dominion and indoctrinated patriarchal ideals.

The quote above illustrates a commonplace trope of women's assumed subjectivity in the postapocalyptic realm that Elison challenges in *The Book of the Unnamed Midwife*. This chapter argues that the preservation of "patriarchal law" is abrogated in the post-apocalyptic realm when motherhood is an apparent impossibility and when the remaining women hold the last threads of hope of avoiding human extinction. In a world where patriarchal hierarchies continue the attempt to possess the only avenue for survival—the maternal body—declining populations of women and the absence of mothers impel the collapse of these assumptions. The re-visioning of maternity in Elison's novel is witnessed and perpetuated through the one practitioner whose pre-apocalypse occupation has seemingly become obsolete: a delivery nurse-midwife. This central character exhibits and promotes gender fluidity; a transformative identity that is manifested in her namelessness; and an intuition with regard to chronicling her own experiences and the experiences of other survivors. All of these characteristics contribute to her fate in ultimately midwifing a newly established social order.

Elison's novel is arranged as a frame story, with the outer frame-narrative set in the distant future, and the primary interior narrative taking place in a future very near our present moment. The distant future depicts a scene in which a number of scribes are learning to carefully rewrite and, thus, preserve an important text: the ancient journals of the "Unnamed Midwife," originally written by the protagonist of the novel. The young male scribes are being taught and directed by a woman who is *eminently* pregnant, and we find out later that it is the exhibition of pregnancy that endows individuals with authority in this new world. The behavior of the young scribes reflects the fact that they "had been trained their whole lives to be silent and obedient to the mothers," which immediately indicates a distinct and purposeful re-visioning of maternity from our non-diegetic reality (3).

The subsequent shift to the past forms the core of the novel, and this primary interior narrative is told in vacillating third-person voice and first-person journal entries. The scene transitions by means of a series of journal entries written by the novel's protagonist, a nurse-midwife who only ever reveals her identity as a series of pseudonyms she adopts as her identity shifts throughout the narrative. In her entries, we see that a terrible disease, a "plague," has struck the population of the United States and the world, and although the death rate is very high for infected men, the women and children who are infected have an approximate two-percent survival rate. Further, there are no successful pregnancies—all babies are stillborn, or the woman miscarries just before succumbing to the plague herself. The protagonist enters the narrative already infected, but manages to survive and develop immunity to the sickness while in a feverish coma.

When she awakens from her comatose state, the Midwife is confronted by a strange man who thought her dead but quickly attempts to rape her. The protagonist, whose first pseudonym is "Karen," fights and kills him, and concludes that she will not be able to avoid another encounter like this one if she does not disguise her female physical characteristics. The Midwife cuts her hair, tapes down her breasts, dresses in "masculine" clothing, and often reminds herself, in a form of mantra: "Walk tall, keep hips straight. Don't sway. Feet flat. Hunch a little, arms straight down . . . . Make fists while talking. Sit with knees apart. Adjust. Don't tilt your head" (30). In this scene, we see the Midwife awaken into an unfamiliar world as a new person with a new gender identity. She has survived the destruction of civilization having developed a resistance to the deadly virus that has focused unremittingly on those like her—women. As a nurse-midwife, she has observed the precipitous decline in birth survival rates and realizes that her entire species is under grave threat, but the plague is not the only threat for surviving women.

The fact that the sickness has centered so explicitly on women, though not a unique trope among post-apocalyptic novels, illustrates the strange transition from the Symbolic order to an upended social structure in *The Book of the Unnamed Midwife*. We see this transition primarily in the manner in which the narrator must adopt a new identity in order to travel freely. Soon after the Plague has felled the un-immune, the few surviving women become commodified as sex slaves for bands of men. "Karen," who has now adopted the name "Rob," knows that any woman she encounters will likely become pregnant if she isn't pregnant already, and pregnancy is a death-sentence due to the omnipresent plague. "Rob," faithful to her obstetric background, raids a clinic and carries with her copious amounts of contraception that she intends to distribute to any women she may encounter. And with this objective in mind, she develops a stratagem that reinforces her new male identity in the eyes of predatory men: she also collects valuable trade-goods such as opiates, cigarettes, and alcohol, which she exchanges for access to enslaved women. Once she is alone with the captive woman, Rob offers life-saving contraception and instructs her on how best to care for herself in this new and terrible world. In this way, Rob presumably saves numerous women's lives.

In this guise of undercover prophylactic dispenser, Rob not only delays the deaths of these few women (though they often die by other means) but also unwittingly preserves the possibility of the renewal of the human race in the future. Due to the frame-narrative arrangement of the novel, we know *a priori* that ultimately women *will* procreate again, which is precisely the author's intent. The narrative does not focus on the question of humanity's survival, but instead on the *means* of its survival when procreation seems impossible and women's fates seem bleak. Further, the brief scene that opens the novel—in which a pregnant woman teaches young men to preserve a woman's now sacred texts—seems entirely unlikely as Rob witnesses women being led in chains. The narrative will center precisely on the difficulty and complexity involved in overturning the pre-catastrophe Symbolic, which occurs by overcoming patriarchal gender assumptions, imbuing maternal characters with agency, and by the queering of burgeoning social communities.

GENDER IDENTITY AND THE INHERENTLY INTERSECTIONAL

Rob experiences internal conflicts and trauma as she grapples with transitioning from her pre-apocalypse identity to one in which she must subdue any indication of her feminine character. It is Rob's experiences and transformation that form the initial focal point of the primary narrative, as this gendered expression becomes a perpetual preoccupation for her whenever she is *en plein aire* and visible to other human beings. As Rob's careful preservation of her masculine guise grows into one of the central concerns of the novel, it becomes more than a means to hide from potential predators. Rob begins to have ancillary internal dialogs, during which she scolds herself in a masculine voice as a constant and painful reminder of the gender that she must exhibit and embody. Early in her journey, Rob is anguished while suppressing her "feminine" affect, and must allow "herself the luxury of a few days' madness. They were dark and deep and held in them the wreck of the entirety of civilization. It crumbles in the individual as it does in the world," (57). The wreck of civilization is acted out metonymically as Rob must destroy her authentic personality to construct a new one fitting for the threatening environment in which she finds herself. These internal dialogs intrude on nearly all of her interactions with other human beings, especially with men—those who have mastered the craft of masculine performance and simultaneously seek out this performance in other presumed men.

The internal dialogs, set apart in italics, detail the struggle to "man-handle" her pre-apocalyptic gender identity. This gender dissonance is echoed in Judith Butler's well-known *Gender Trouble*. The text is named, in part, after the "trouble" Butler observed was encountered universally in woman's experience, trouble that "euphemized some fundamentally mysterious problem usually related to the alleged mystery of all things feminine," (vii). Rob finds herself in "trouble" as she re/cognizes herself as a phallogocentrist subject by disassembling and contriving her gendered subjectivity and then turning that lens on *herself*. In all of her interactions Rob still sees herself as the subject of desire, of the masculine gaze, and yet must possess and mobilize that same gaze despite the emotional alienation this brings about. Gender is fluid, and

> relative to the constructed relations in which it is determined. As a shifting and contextual phenomenon, gender does not denote a substantive being, but a relative point of convergence among culturally and historically specific sets of relations. (Butler, *Trouble*, 10)

The Midwife reveals throughout the narrative that she has never ascribed to any specific gender definition, and when she is confronted by a heteronormative person who doesn't understand the protagonist's bisexuality, she explains that "I like people. They come with the bodies they come with" (Elison, 214). Yet, she finds herself compelled to engage in a complicated "masquerade [that] may be understood as the performative production of a sexual ontology, an appearing that makes itself convincing as a 'being,'" but the ontological production is a contrivance that the Midwife finds she can barely maintain (Butler, *Trouble*, 47). For example, when she first encounters her future traveling companion, Roxanne, the older woman is leashed on a chain, nearly naked. Rob approaches the men holding the leash, and the internal dialog begins: "*Secure. Totally secure. A little selfish*," (63, original italics). These self-directed commands inform her masquerade so that she may portray a masculinity that will maintain her safety and gain her access to the enslaved women. Yet her mask slips, just slightly, when she hears something shocking or disturbing, as when the men holding Roxanne say that they intend to journey to Central America because there are "lots more women down there" (63). Rob then redirects her thoughts to "*Lots of women. Also milk and honey, and the streets are paved with gold*," (63). By internally reciting these mantras of clichéd manhood, Rob is able to continue to engage in trade talk for the women slaves, and thus find ways to medicate them, reassure them, and sometimes even free them. Rob learns to embody the masculine gaze, invoke it when necessary, and employ it for the benefit of the few remaining women she encounters.

This "macho" self-talk eventually becomes an inveterate counterpoint to her own "authentic" reveries, and leads to contention between the identity Rob is struggling to cultivate and the one that she has formed over the entirety of her pre-apocalyptic life. This internal conflict between her gendered selves, what Butler describes as a form of melancholy, takes place, for example, as she prepares herself to vacate a house that she has occupied for the winter and re-enter the threatening world outside:

> *Put on all the weight I can, and my biceps look so developed = wish I could go sleeveless to show everyone how manly I am . . .*
> *Mannish. Perfect.*
> *. . . Cut my hair and brushed my beard on again. Early spring = tulips already out by the lake. . . . Only had to kill. Didn't have to. Did. Can't think about that.* (58, original italics)

In this journal entry, Rob's painstaking effort to appear "mannish" stems from desperation to perform masculinity that is intertwined with contrived ambivalence toward life—a thought process that is antithetical to her former role as midwife. As her thoughts turn toward the flowers emerging with the spring, her guilt over committing murder surfaces more insistently as she attempts to quell it. Yet this "effeminate" reaction can be a threat to her safety and to the tenuous grip that Rob holds with regard to her new masculinized subjectivity.

The cutting of Rob's hair and brushing on of the beard completes this image, both external and internal, for the Midwife. Because the novel is largely based on Rob's journal entries and thus her internal thoughts and reactions, the narrative makes clear that the focus for much of the novel is not the external world of the post-apocalypse, or on how Rob is seen by other survivors. The novel functions as an examination of the transformation of gender-circumscribed Symbolic, one centered in the lone perspective of a woman trained to deliver new life from women's bodies. As a woman operating as a man, who values the lives of women *not* for their potential for sexual pleasure and impregnation but rather to prevent their deaths and mitigate their suffering, the Midwife undermines common assumptions about post-apocalypse maternal female characters. As the narrative progresses, she will witness—and take part in—the upending of the Symbolic through which she is trying to survive.

Barbara Katz Rothman, in her essay "Beyond Mothers and Fathers: Ideology in a Patriarchal Society" (1994), argues that our cultural understanding of motherhood in the United States (and the West) is a self-contradictory one in which mothers historically function as little more than the ground in which the patriarch's seed may be planted, and

> paternity is the central social relationship . . . in the *Book of Genesis*, in the "begats." Each man, from Adam onward, is described as having "begat a son in his likeness." . . . In a patriarchal kinship system, children are born to men, out of women. (141)

Rothman accurately describes the conventional values of most post-apocalyptic novels—the potential for reproduction seems to be a central concern in novels in which women of childbearing age appear and where they are tasked with regenerating the population by whatever means necessary. This fixation with reproduction is enacted by men without consultation with the women themselves, as is glaringly apparent in such novels as Margaret Atwood's *The Handmaid's Tale* (1985), in which women are systematically subjugated for state-sponsored exploitation of their uterus. This exploitation is also evident in Elison's novel, in which we see a scene where a young woman is captured and impregnated, and the apparent father quickly claims the unborn child for himself, without regard for what the pregnancy will mean for her. The Midwife learns of this pregnancy from a distance, but the recounting of this horrifying episode entrenches the Midwife's goal to prevent as many pregnancies as possible in order to safeguard the possible return of maternity. Elison places the protagonist in this conventional exploitative context in order for her to experience the upending of post-apocalyptic patriarchy and participate in the new maternal future.

SILENT MOTHER AND THE STILL, STILL BORN

One of the most harrowing scenes in the novel is centered on a young woman named Shawna, a fourteen-year-old who is captured by a band of men and raped repeatedly. She soon discovers that she is pregnant and, due to the Plague, realizes that she likely has only months to live. The significance of this episode is twofold. For one, this episode elaborates on the idea of the silent maternal body that is a central trope in post-apocalypse novels and in maternal theory. Second, this scene brings to light the violence and horror of what is only insinuated in numerous other apocalyptic novels, in which the impregnation and enslavement of women is considered a foregone and concomitant element of the post-apocalypse landscape. The true violence of this form of victimization is rarely critically depicted.

The narrative introduces Shawna through Roxanne's diary entry. Roxanne is a woman that the Midwife, now calling herself Alex, briefly befriends. Roxanne is a slave to a band of men when she first sees Shawna wandering down a road entirely unarmed and oblivious to danger, "not even hiding" (Elison, 77). This is unusual, as enough time has passed after the catastrophic plague that it does not seem possible this young woman could have escaped capture up to this point. And yet, when Roxanne has the opportunity to speak to Shawna, Roxanne recalls "she had been a virgin, she told me crying" (78). The strangeness and horror of this episode are further underscored by the onset of her plague symptoms: "After a few weeks, [Shawna] was throwing up every morning and getting tired enough to crash in the early afternoon. . . . She thought she had the fever after all" (78). Shawna, the once wandering virgin, is now pregnant, and unbeknownst to the small group, is fated soon to die. The incessant gang rapes cease, and the men in the group forage for offerings to bring to the pregnant Shawna, including rare foods that the women were not allowed to have before.

However, despite the new reverence Shawna receives from the men in the group, she remains quiet and without autonomy: "Shawna barely knew what it meant or what would happen. She had no kind of guess about the father, and she was afraid of all of them" (78). Aaron, the self-proclaimed leader of the group, soon claims Shawna and the baby as his own, and "started calling her 'prized possession' or 'pride and joy.' [Shawna] didn't see the good in it. . . . She had no preferences, just terror" (78). Shawna thus embodies a number of characteristics often associated with the pregnant slave trope of post-apocalyptic novels, such as passivity, submission, and silence.

The young Shawna further exhibits characteristics of what Michelle Boulous Walker refers to as the silent maternal body. In her book, *Philosophy and the Maternal Body: Reading Silence*, Walker describes the silencing of the maternal body as emerging from early in the history of Western philosophy:

> Plato's parable of the cave . . . [a]t one and the same time constructs the maternal body, and then proceeds to appropriate it for its own ends. . . . In Plato's world woman . . . remains silent, reduced to the mute passivity of her reproductive role. (Walker, 12)

Walker focuses on the necessity to acknowledge the "repressed maternal body" that inhabits Western thought and writing, manifested in a "silence [that] entails a spoken yet unheard voice . . . [T]his readable absence or unheard voice is structured by a logic of repression. Repression is a process that is closely tied to denial" (Walker, 27). This repression and appropriation take place in the possession of Shawna, who serves as a paradigm both for all such appropriated women that the Midwife seeks to rescue, and the enslaved pregnant women and mothers that so often appear in post-apocalyptic fiction. Shawna serves as a means to deconstruct these silent figures that conventionally form as fundamental an aspect of the post-catastrophe landscape as disintegrating buildings and roadside corpses.

Shawna thus embodies a number of characteristics often associated with not only the pregnant slave trope in post-apocalyptic novels, but a sort of Marian character that functions as a self-sacrificing or long-suffering maternal figure characterized by her virginity and voicelessness. Julia Kristeva describes this character as a "virginal Maternal," and as a Marian character Shawna exhibits what Kristeva describes as "the postulate . . . attained only through an exacerbated masochism: a concrete woman, worthy of the feminine ideal embodied by the Virgin" (Kristeva, "Mater," 149). Shawna fits this feminine ideal as one who is abused, is a youth, is quiet and "concrete," and petrified by terror. She is an extreme embodiment of what Walker points out is the common portrayal of a "phallic maternal," the

> mother who scarcely knows her own desire; the de-sexualized mother of masculine mythology. Her sexuality simply does not exist beyond her reproductive potential. . . . The contradictory logics of production and (sexual) reproduction are contained within her mute and silenced body. (Walker, 136)

Although Shawna is graphically portrayed as someone with whom the men have sex, she exhibits no desire, is never given a choice, and is thus bent to the "values of production" even before having the chance to understand what pleasure might mean (Walker, 135). This trope of the productive phallic maternal, so commonplace in post-apocalyptic fiction, is one that Elison critiques through Shawna. Mary O'Brien, in her book *The Politics of Reproduction,* points out that

> we cannot analyse reproduction from the standpoint of any existing theory. The theories themselves are products of male-stream thought. . . . What we must therefore do is turn to the fundamental biological process in which reproductive relations are grounded and subject it to analysis from a female perspective. (24)

This is precisely the theoretical lens that Elison has centered on conventional maternal characters in post-apocalypse novels: by re-focusing on post-catastrophe reproduction from a *female* perspective, the author undermines and critiques the view that "the patriarchy was not a historical institution but a 'prehistorical,' natural arrangement" (O'Brien, 25). Shawna is the embodiment of this patriarchal Symbolic post-apocalyptic trope, and her presence is necessary for Elison to later turn the Symbolic on its head and establish a maternal post-apocalypse.

As a point of comparison, one may look to the post-apocalypse portrayed in the paradigmatic 1985 novel *The Postman,* which includes a number of Marian phallic maternal characters. One of these women is held by the Holnists, wild men who embody the post-apocalyptic trope of male characters who have embraced their "primitive tendencies," forming "bands of the white-camouflaged barbarians roaming the countryside, burning small hamlets and dragging off food, women, slaves" (186). In one scene, the trope of the Marian maternal ideal is embodied in a nameless woman who functions as a martyr on behalf of her son:

> These postwar crazies had taken to raiding for women, as well as for food and slaves. After the first few years of slaughter, most Holnist enclaves had found themselves with incredibly high male-female ratios. Now, women were valuable chattel in the loose, macho, hyper-survivalist societies. . . . No wonder some of the raiders below wanted to carry this one back. Gordon could tell that she might be quite pretty, if she healed and if the pall of terror ever left her eyes. The boy in her arms watched the men with fierce anger. (Brin, 107)

Here, the woman being held by the Holnists is further objectified by the protagonist, Gordon, who does not see her reality as one of enslavement and repeated rape. Rather, he views her as a potential beauty, if only she would cease to exhibit her unattractive terror-stricken visage. How would Gordon see her if, instead of terror, her face was twisted with the rage, that her son exhibits? Marianne Hirsch states in her book *Mother / Daughter Plot: Narrative, Psychoanalysis, Feminism* that "the course of a maternal representation . . . seems still to be shaped by a cultural imaginary that participates in and underwrites unconscious fears of the maternal," and thus would be inappropriate for a potential object of desire (40). Would it not be more fitting if this unnamed mother were to exhibit the rage that is, instead, expressed by her son? Or would that anger erase entirely the possibility that she may be "quite pretty," and thus worth rescuing? In the midst of this ordeal, "Gordon put a finger to his lips. . . . The woman blinked, and Gordon *feared for a moment she was about to speak*" (Brin, 108, emphasis added). Of course, this fear emerges as Gordon attempts to avoid drawing the attention of the Holnists, but the fear of her maternal voice, and its potential rage, is where a deeper patriarchal fear resides.

In protecting her child, the woman only displays a look of terror, while her son expresses rage at the men who are debating whether or not to kill the woman and child. This absence of anger, the repression of maternal rage, is characteristic of what Kristeva deems the Marian vision of the "virginal Maternal," a repressive image often "seen taking shape in the Western symbolic economy" through literary culture, among other outlets ("Stabat," 143–144). The portrayal of mothers who conspicuously lack anger in the face of exploitation and abuse is not solely an attribute of post-apocalyptic fiction, of course. The avoidance of the portrayal of maternal anger is a conventional proclivity in the Western imaginary, as Hirsch states. This "unnatural" maternal anger emerges from what Hirsch refers to as maternal subjectivity, a form of agency that must be repressed, since "maternal anger is depicted as powerful and threatening. Such figurations necessarily shape maternal representations and self-representations. . . . [E]ven in post-modern feminist fiction, maternal stories are mediated and suppressed, especially if they involve anger" (39). The unnamed woman of Brin's novel is not a character from a feminist fiction, to be sure, but nevertheless epitomizes the absence of maternal anger, and exhibits instead "Marian pain [that] is in no way connected with tragic outburst" (Kristeva, "Stabat," 144). The same may be said of Shawna who, after her capture and almost perpetual rape, succumbs to fear and deafening silence. The striking difference between these two characters is the narrative lens in which each is placed: one is a tragic Marian character who maintains the image of the "Maternal Virgin" as she sacrifices herself for her son; though fighting by scratching, she is never described as angry, even dying with an expression of "reverence, loyalty, and a confident faith in ultimate redemption"; her body untouched by the men who previously violated her, despite their threats to do so again (Brin, 108). Shawna, on the other hand, is a passive and silent victim of explicit rape, whose voicelessness is presumably appropriate within the horrifying context in which she has been forcibly placed. However, though her story is told by another woman, a fellow slave, the storyteller never exhibits more than sarcastic annoyance in the recollection of Shawna's abuse and, by proxy, her own.

The fact that mothers, even in the speculative landscape of the post-apocalypse are so often portrayed as expressionless enslaved victims or as unresistant rape-survivors is indicative of the degree to which this fear of maternal rage is entrenched even in post-apocalyptic literature. The paucity of motherly anger in the emerging genre of maternal post-apocalyptic novels is conspicuous when considered alongside conventional post-apocalyptic texts. As numerous post-apocalyptic novels include rape and domination of women as a matter of course in their narratives, female characters lose autonomy and become possessions of men without question or with feeble resistance, and often may only escape through death. In Cormac McCarthy's 2006 novel *The Road*, the spouse of the unnamed male protagonist concludes that this is her reality. Despite her spouse's refusal to acknowledge her grave certainty, her acquiescence to an inescapable future as a sexual victim is the impetus for her subsequent suicide. She insists: "Sooner or later they will catch and they will kill us. They will rape me. They'll rape [our child]. They are going to rape us and kill us and eat us" (56). Because there is no possibility of resistance, she leaves the post-apocalyptic landscape in the only manner possible for her. Later in the narrative, the protagonist witnesses precisely what his spouse had predicted, when he sees women being led along with other slaves, "perhaps a dozen in number, some of them [visibly] pregnant" (78). The women are restrained in a herd-like group, shackled, in a scene that is not unusual in post-apocalyptic novels.

When female characters exhibit resistance to their oppression, some narratives admonish these women through sexual punishment. In Margaret Atwood's post-apocalyptic novel, *Maddaddam* (2013), the final novel in a post-apocalyptic trilogy, the character Amanda is kidnapped by small band of violent men and is repeatedly raped and ultimately impregnated. In the previous novels of the trilogy, Amanda is portrayed as incorrigible, determined never to be subject to anyone, particularly men. However, in the final novel, Amanda's extensive enslavement to the "Painballers," characters similar to David Brin's "Holnists," leaves her voiceless and cringing after Ren and the other more valorous survivors finally rescue her:

> They'd been tracking Ren's best friend, and they'd found her just in time because the two Painballers who'd been using her had almost used her up. Toby was familiar with the ways of such men: she'd almost been killed by one of them. . . . Anyone who'd survived Painball more than once had been reduced to a Reptilian brain. Sex until you were worn to a fingernail was their mode. (9)

Despite the fact that the men who kidnap Amanda are portrayed as anomalous, the entire trilogy suggests that this treatment of women, as absent of agency and silent property of men, is an unsurprising fate. This is particularly true for women who are capable of childbearing, which is why Toby, raped but unable to bear children, survives with her personality intact, while Amanda, who becomes pregnant, remains "so traumatized she was almost catatonic" (Atwood, 10). This hierarchy of abusive maternal potentiality is established early in the trilogy as the character Toby finds herself in the possession of the restaurant owner Blanco, who rapes her and claims her as his possession, as he has previously done to numerous other women who worked for him. Toby, having endured treatment similar to Amanda, becomes one of the most resilient characters by the trilogy's conclusion. Amanda, on the other hand, never truly recovers, and from the moment of her rescue and impregnation, never exhibits anger or assertiveness again. Although Toby and Amanda have endured similar abuses, Amanda's impregnation seems to be a punishment for her previous recalcitrance, whereas Toby's loss of her family drives her both into abuse and out of it, and yet she grows increasingly self-assured. This pattern of the silencing of the maternal appears similarly in the relationship between Shawna and the woman who tells her story, Roxanne. Whereas Shawna is a young woman capable of bearing children, Roxanne reveals: "I'd had a hysterectomy" (Elison, 77). Both Shawna and Roxanne experience similar abuse by the same group of men, but impregnated Shawna is left voiceless and dies before ever having the opportunity to tell her own story. Roxanne is able to tell her own story and Shawna's, and chooses to accompany and then abandon the Midwife when the moment suits her. Similarly, the unnamed mother in *The Postman* dies before she can recount her experiences, leaving her son to carry on with Gordon.

The inclusion of the element of silent domination of maternal women is such a common trope that it seems almost standard in post-apocalyptic fiction. Yet, rarely do any of these novels closely examine the violent act of domination and victimization, whether by rape or physical abuse, almost never actually portraying the horror faced by the women who are captured. The episode of Shawna's enslavement is a stark means of confronting systemic narrative domination and silencing of women, taking this trope out of the realm of fantasy and post-apocalyptic implicit normativity and exposing it for all to observe. The narrative details Shawna's abuse takes the violence out of the imaginary and into an explicit and grotesque reality. Yet, this exploitation goes even further by including the fact that the possibility of impregnation will result in Shawna's death. This episode is recounted by Roxanne, who admits she did not know at the time that the Plague was still present:

> Chuck and Ethan raided a drugstore and came back with a test. She peed on the stick, and lo and behold. The guys put their heads together about everything they had heard about babies and the fever. More than one of them had heard that all the kids born during the shitstorm had died. They all agreed that none of us had the fever, so the kid couldn't get it . . . I don't know fucking anything about birthing no babies . . . neither did the guys. (78–79)

Here, we see the importance of midwifery for the future possibility of human live births. A nearly full-term pregnancy and subsequent labor is such a rarity that each occurrence opens up the anticipation of possible human survival. But the men who enslave Shawna and the other women slaves are only able to look on as Shawna goes into labor, in agony as the both the laboring pangs and plague symptoms take hold:

> Out of nowhere, Shawna heated up. . . . Her face and joints were hot to the touch . . . Shawna bore down, and I saw the kid's head. . . . The kid came out all in a rush. . . . The baby was in my hands, tiny and thin. He didn't move or breathe. . . . He was blotchy and blue and never drew a breath . . . Shawna lay limp on the floor, still bleeding out and turning white. . . . After a while, Aaron laid the baby down in Shawna's arms, and we left. . . . The chains went back on. Nobody talked about Shawna or the baby. (79–80)

This scene, occurring in the first third of the novel, makes immediately clear that rape victims in the post-apocalypse landscape will not be viewed from a distance. Shawna, unlike the unnamed woman of *The Postman*, nor Amanda of *Madaddam*, nor the women from *The Road*, or any other post-apocalyptic novel, illustrates from beginning to end the reality of the portrayal of women as silent sexual slaves. Further, the prospect of motherhood in the post-apocalyptic landscape has perpetuated women's voicelessness. However, in the case of Shawna, the commonplace trope of the pregnant female victim is unveiled, revealing the horror and violence that is never truly explored in other novels that include this trope. In bringing to bear the terror of sexual enslavement and impregnation, Elison presses upon the dispassionate inclusion of such tropes in the post-apocalyptic landscape, and in so doing opens the way forward for the possibility of new ways of viewing maternity that do not necessitate enslavement and violence. The narrative of *The Unnamed Midwife* acts out the possibility of this genre-wide transformation in many ways. One of the most significant transitions occurs in a microcosm of pre-apocalyptic Symbolic through a hermetic religious colony that the Midwife discovers as she journeys away from her brief partnership with Roxanne.

THE COLONY AND COLLAPSE OF PATRIARCHAL MATERNITY

Much of the second half of the novel is centered on the first fixed settlement that Rob has encountered since she began her circuitous journey. Rob, now calling herself Dusty, first realizes that "something was different here" when "she began to see cows fenced in on suburban lawns in twos and threes. . . . [S]he heard the unmistakable gabbling of a chicken coop. She immediately knew people were keeping the animals," (106). Indeed, she does find a settlement of people here, a "survivor's colony and a stake of the Church of Jesus Christ of Latter-Day Saints" (109). Dusty's encounter with a Mormon colony in the town of Huntsville may seem initially unusual in the post-apocalyptic landscape, but the settlement's existence points to an already changing way of life. There is a distinct focus on Dusty's interactions with the colony, making up a large portion of the narrative, signifying a larger transformation from the Symbolic to a form of society in which patriarchal norms are increasingly nonexistent.

This religious enclave has preserved its pre-apocalyptic patriarchal hierarchy, and it is precisely due to the unquestioned fundamentalism of the Mormon members that this system could possibly be realistically preserved in this decimated world. If there were any acts of resistance or rebellion, this hierarchy would fall apart, as will soon become apparent. Yet, at this point, the narrative makes clear that this potential site of hope for the future of mankind is based on the fallacious premise that pre-apocalyptic structures can be maintained. As we witness through Dusty's eyes, the enforcement of patriarchal law on a dwindling society cannot be sustained. The contrived disempowerment of the few remaining women is central to this community's collapse. In order for any semblance of society to thrive, new communities must come to terms with the decimation of the Symbolic, and must construct a new way forward that is not based on pre-apocalyptic patriarchal ideology.

When Dusty first arrives and is invited to share a meal with the inhabitants of the colony, she sees the women: there are three of them, one perhaps twenty years old, another in her thirties, and an older, graying woman: maiden, mother, and crone. This triad of hope for the future dutifully serves food to the men, and Dusty "felt insanely awkward. . . . Their whole society looked like pretense to her, like a stubborn conceit. *Let's pretend we have a community. Let's pretend nothing has changed*" (114, original emphasis). Dusty discovers that the women are not only responsible for carrying out most food preparation, but must also care for four children who have survived the plague. Dusty attempts to speak to them as

> they were pulling long muffin trays out of a large wall oven. . . . The woman with the gray at her temples set down her corn muffins . . . 'I'm Sister Everly . . . I'm afraid that's all the speaking we're going to do without our husbands present. (120–121)

Soon after, Dusty is reprimanded by one of the village elders for "flirting" with the women, and is asked to leave. The elder, named Comstock, does ask that Dusty remain in residence just outside of the community, in case of medical need. There is a clear puritanical conservative ideology that is strictly maintained at the expense of these women's freedom. Kristeva's concept of the Marian maternal is also at work, serving as the feminine ideal and exemplified by the

> incredible construct of the Maternal that the West elaborated by means of the Virgin, and . . . women's wishes for identification as well as the very precise interposition of those who assumed to keep watch over the symbolic and social order. ("Stabat,"147)

As the narrative reveals, this ideal is, indeed, a construct, one that collapses when the symbolic and social order can no longer be maintained.

There is very little consideration of possible independence for the female inhabitants in this strictly indoctrinated colony, and as Dusty explores the community in the brief time that she is allowed, she finds that this seemingly solid stringent settlement is built on an unstable framework. One of the young men with whom Dusty will share a room, Chet, describes the painful contrast he feels between the life before the apocalypse and his present reality. He states that

> every family I knew in Ogden had daughters, more girls than boys . . . I miss them so much, all of them. I keep hoping the missionaries will bring back a bunch of girls. . . . But most of the guys who leave don't even come back. (117)

Chet mentions the role of the "missionaries" of the community, and it is this obligatory vocation that reveals the intensely brutal ideology sustaining the post-apocalyptic settlement. Dusty later asks Comstock about Chet's disappeared roommate.

> "Do you lose a lot of people that way?"
> . . . "A few, yes."
> . . . She struggled for a minute, not sure what to say.
> "Oh. Suicides . . . That's happening everywhere. You know that, right? Living this way is hard. People are going to opt out. . . . You should tell Chet. . . . He needs to know it's over. Everyone does."
> "No." He shook his head . . .
> *He doesn't want anyone to know. Bad for leadership, bad for morale. Unsustainable.*
> "How many?"
> "It's not important. It's going to stop the minute we find just one more woman or girl out there. That will be enough to bring hope. She will come. She was promised to us" (130–131, original italics).

This promised "Eve," an illusion perpetuated to maintain the tenuous system of "missionary work," is built on a patriarchal order that Comstock admits is maintained only by solicitous fiat of the inhabitants. The three women survivors are compelled to serve the men due to their presumed lower order in the social hierarchy. The men are sent away from the community for an apparent noble cause, but one from which they are unlikely to survive—a dark form of male-population control. The disturbing discussion between Dusty and Comstock reveals the lack of value placed on men's lives, as expendable and "not important." These lives are disposable even as the overall population is dwindling, in order to seek out just one woman, a mythical Mary figure who will supposedly usher in a new future. But the treatment of the women already living in the colony, as well as the implicit possession of a woman "promised to us" suggests that this hope is reserved only for men like Comstock, men in power who assert ownership over the female inhabitants and send the male rivals to their deaths. Further, the promised Eve-Mary is an imaginary figure that is consonant with her biblical counterpart as described by Sandra Gilbert and Susan Gubar: "Eve is humbled by becoming a slave not only to Adam the individual man but to Adam the archetypal man, a slave not only to her husband but . . . to the species" (Gilbert and Gubar, 197). This hierarchical symbolic assures the male inhabitants that any woman who will enter into the community will enter a life of servitude, and like Eve, her daughters will foster the human species in servitude and confinement.

Despite the apparent impetus for this mythical quest, the hunt for an Eve is unsurprisingly futile, and Dusty tries to convince Chet and others of this. She sees the larger picture, and based on her experiences "outside," she understands very well the doomed fate of the inhabitants of the community:

> "*He has to see the situation. The logic is so simple.*
> 'Look, there are too many men here, and not enough women. Didn't it occur to you that the elders are trying to get rid of you?'
> Chet looked hurt. 'Why would they do that? . . . '
> 'Because sooner or later you're going to fight over the women. There will be affairs. Unless more women join you, it's inevitable. The elders are just trying to even up the score' . . .
> 'The point is to do what God wills. That's all. . . .
> *They don't know. They haven't really seen what it's like out there, and there's no way to tell them.*" (135, original italics)

This discussion reveals to Dusty that her attempts to save these men's lives are hopeless. Chet not only mentions that his former roommate "disappeared," but that others in the community are losing hope and "disappearing," and the only chance they may have lies in the four survivor children, "two boys, two girls. All under ten . . . they're in a special house. . . . They have to be protected" (118). Dusty is dismayed to learn that the children are isolated from the rest of the community, and knows that this arrangement may endanger them even more, leaving them vulnerable "*hidden children. Flowers in the attic*" (118). This surreal arrangement, in which children and women remain isolated and constrained, is untenable. Yet, Chet refuses to consider this reality, and instead intones the conviction of those in the community that "those kids can marry each other. . . . They're the only thing we have that looks like a future" (118). However, when Dusty later looks at a wall display of the survivor children's artwork,

> Dusty thought they were probably directed by an adult. Every picture . . . envisioned a perfect world. If children of the plague were allowed to draw what

they felt, Dusty imagined the room would look different. But all the children's pictures had smiling mommies in them. (121)

This display reveals the misguided preoccupation of the community members: the tiny hands that hold their society's future also depict it centered in the existence of mothers. The display of these child-drawn images is meant to renew hope for the colonists, but the message they depict is so entirely severed from reality that they seem to have emerged from a collective delusion. Yet, Dusty finds herself continually astonished by the fictional reality that the colony inhabitants have constructed, which appears a far greater fantasy than even the children have depicted.

Through mutual agreement, Dusty will live outside of the compound, and once she has left the settlement to live on her own, she believes she will have little interaction with the surreal colonists in the future. Dusty has chosen to live in a nearby town called Eden—a reference to the author's inverse analogy to the biblical Genesis. Then one evening, Jodi, the youngest of the three surviving women, travels through driving snow in the dark to plead for Dusty's help. In the brief time that Dusty spends time with Jodi, she learns that her predictions have come true and the community is collapsing over possession of its female inhabitants. One of the "missionaries," Brother Danielson, did find a surviving woman in good health and brought her back to the settlement. However, instead of being the Marian Eve savior that would inaugurate a new phase of hope and contentment, the woman's appearance sparks desperation and infighting among those who do not have wives—which is, of course, the vast majority of the male inhabitants. Danielson announces that the new woman would be his wife and that she is already pregnant with his child. Yet, the other inhabitants insist that they should have a chance to "court" her, compelling Danielson to state he would protect his "prize" by lethal means. The promised Eve has arrived, complete with the apparent next human generation in gestation, but she is firmly in Danielson's possession.

However, unlike the biblical mother of human genesis, Danielson's spouse does not carry *life* in utero, but death. According to biblical lore, "Eve's . . . fall completes the human entry into generation, since its consequence is the pain of birth, death's necessary and opposite mirror image . . ." (Gilbert and Gubar, 197). Yet, this pregnant woman seems to instead embody the pain of human eschatology, and her decline is rather an embodiment of death than generation of its opposite—death of the fetus, herself, and the settlement. She is soon consumed with plague symptoms, which infects several others who are somehow not immune, including the children. One of the original three women dies, and three of the children die, leaving one nine-year-old girl whose immunity to the plague has saved her. The colony-wide degeneration continues as Bishop Comstock also dies, leaving a man named Bishop Graves as the community's leader. Graves announces his claim over and marriage to the surviving nine-year-old girl, Patty. The other surviving female, Sister Johannsen, is compelled to remarry, and Jodi herself is commanded to do the same. Jodi reveals to the Midwife that "Brother Graves turned on me. He said that my husband is never coming back, that God showed it to him. He said I needed to remarry" (146). The sudden further decline in women has brought about an even harsher patriarchal law than before, and Jodi reveals Graves's declaration that "women would be given in marriage by their fathers or by the bishop from now on. Period. We don't get to decide anymore" (146). The patristic dominion over female autonomy is entire, completing their transformation from potential Eves to subjugated chattel.

These scenes of the colony's disintegration are significant for the novel's larger portrayal of the collapse of the Symbolic in the post-Apocalyptic world. The careful organization and strict hierarchy based on pre-Apocalyptic patriarchal order formed the framework for this self-sufficient settlement, and following Dusty's previous journey through the plague-decimated landscape, this colony seemed to hold the greatest certainty for humanity's survival. Yet Dusty's own experience on the "outside," in both the post- *and* pre-apocalyptic worlds, has given her an insight that underscores her role as a sort of "wise woman" who resides outside of all patriarchal norms. As a midwife, this character operates within an unacknowledged and historically disparaged genealogy, one that Adrienne Rich describes as historically "synonymous with dirt, ignorance, and superstition," yet the Midwife is simultaneously recognized for her sagacity, since "for several centuries, the knowledge of pregnancy, of the birth-process, of female anatomy, and of methods for facilitating labor, was being accumulated entirely by women," and passed on by generations of midwives (Rich, 135). The character of Dusty, who remains unnamed throughout the narrative, embodies the history of these sage women whose knowledge has been lost, since they

> did not write books; and the real history of the development of birthing as an art . . . is blotted out in the history of male obstetrics . . . the names of the great midwives are mostly lost. (Rich, 134)

The exception, in Dusty's case, is that she *does* ultimately write a treatise that will preserve her legacy of a new form of midwifery.

The nameless midwife, kindred to the childless female in this novel, is a trope that the narrative explores in-depth when Dusty has a conversation with the character Honus, the temporarily absent father of the fetus that Sister Jodi Obermeyer carries. Honus has finally returned, and he and the Midwife work together to acquire resources for their survival. Dusty and Honus are alone together on one of these missions to acquire supplies for the impending birth, and he asks her "But don't you want to have kids?" (198). Dusty emphasizes her childless role as midwife, answering, "I caught kids for a living. I got the miracle of life on a daily basis. That was enough," (198). Of course, this answer does not placate the staunchly paternal and patriarchally traditional Honus, who insists that delivering children is "not the same as having kids of your own" (198). Dusty halts discussion of the idealization of childbearing by directing Honus to the reality of their new world, stating, "Let's wait and see how Jodi's birth goes. Let's see if anyone survives childbirth ever again. Ok?" (199). Though Honus does not realize this, his next question points to her embodied history as a midwife: "Is your name really Dusty?" (199). Not only is this an attempt to re-appropriate the identity of the Midwife by "possessing" her name, the question is a play on the ancient history of this lineage of unnamed women: does your real name reside among the deleterious dusty and lost annals of antiquity? Dusty acknowledges that this is not her "real name," but this acknowledgment is accompanied by an increasingly familiar emotion: "She felt it again, that same tug of meaning, of power attached to her real name. She could give him another fake, but that would only complicate things with Jodi. She looked at him and felt drawn in, felt the ghost of their bodies pressed together on the ride into town" (199). The power that is associated with the possible revelation of her name is undoubtedly sexual in nature but also, as stated here, implies another "tug of meaning, of power" that is embodied in her identity that remains in her possession. This implicit power elicits the famous phrase by Simone de Beauvoir, that "one is not born, but rather becomes, woman," and the protection of her pre-apocalyptic name insulates Dusty from the threat of re-instituting adamic naming (and creative) power over her impregnable identity (Beauvoir, 283). By remaining anonymously Dusty, the unnamed Midwife retains full control and sovereignty over how the male re/cognizes her, and how she is cognizant of her nebulous gender identity and "abnormality" through his eyes.

The question of the Midwife's namelessness follows a Western convention of not just unknown midwives, but the historical ambivalence of social legitimacy for women. Sandra Gilbert and Susan Gubar trace this practice through their analysis of Mary Shelley and her Frankenstein's monster, who "may really be a female monster in disguise" (237). The fe/male monster is defined in part by "social illegitimacy, his bastardy, his namelessness . . . he is himself as nameless as a woman is in patriarchal society" (241). The Midwife carries this social illegitimacy and ambivalence with her when faced with Honus, the narrative's paradigm of patriarchal ideology and cognizance. Honus is perpetually flummoxed by Dusty, from the very first moment that he finds out Dusty is not the man she convinced the Mormons she was, but a woman, and he looks at her with disgust. Up to the moment she insists on leaving, and he cannot comprehend her lack of affection for him: "I knew you loved me. . . . He smiled like a man who knows he has won . . . [Dusty responded,] 'This is like helping a kitten get out of a tree. It's not love, it's pity" (248). The Midwife does not behave in a way that is recognizable to Honus, and Dusty embraces his perception of her monstrousness by refusing to ever reveal her birth name, by having sex joyously, and by rejecting the implicit "duty" to attempt to give birth. The series of pseudonyms that the Midwife adopts reflects her gender fluidity by creating a narrative of its own: unnamed, Karen, Carl, Alex, Dusty, and ultimately Jane. From Karen, a conventional female name in the United States, to Carl and Alex, both German and Greek words for "man"; Dusty is a moniker that points to the Midwife's increasing gender and identity indistinction; and her final name, Jane, is a woman unidentified: "Jane Doe." By refusing to ever reveal her pre-apocalyptic name, the Midwife challenges the presumed "problem of names and their connection with social legitimacy" with regard to identity, thus further diminishing the efficacy of the patriarchal Symbolic that seeks to reimpose this convention on women survivors (Gilbert and Gubar, 241).

Thus, Dusty's unnamed state, as well as her critical ordeal in witnessing her profession literally and figuratively dying in her arms with the onset of the plague, demonstrates not only the decimation of the human population but also its diminishing ability to maintain the patriarchal hold over the process of maternity. Dusty represents the ancient knowledge of women that has returned enraged, as ancient as the biblical midwives Puah and Shifrah who were incorrigible in preserving their province of deliverers of life rather than carrying out the mortal wrath of paternal law[1]. Dusty is a supportive listener for Honus and Jodi, and as she listens to Jodi's accounts of her former community, she "was boiling with an old anger. It seemed as old as the world," (146). Dusty is hearing the monstrous final desperate gasps of patriarchal order in its attempt to possess and bind the last diminishing maternal lives, eliciting the "old anger" of generations of women whose crucial vocation was centered in empowering women to push through the most difficult physical, and likely most emotionally intense moments of their lives. The midwives persisted in carrying out their service despite the ever-burgeoning "male prejudice and the power of a male-dominated establishment to discredit and drive out even the most talented women practitioners" (Rich, 142). However, we see that Dusty's role is to revitalize this diminished profession in the post-Symbolic, and in so doing, instantiate a new landscape of maternal rather than paternal ascendancy.

Jodi's appearance on Dusty's doorstep in the town of Eden presents another challenge, beyond Jodi's escape from the threat of compulsory remarriage (read re-enslavement). To Dusty's shock and horror, Jodi is pregnant with her husband's child. Her pregnancy was hidden from the rest of the community, which saves her from possible further isolation and subjugation. Yet, of course, there is a very serious issue that accompanies all pregnancies in this new world: they are fatal for the fetus and, likely, the mother. Dusty broaches the subject soon after Jodi's arrival, but the pregnant woman firmly states,

> "That doesn't matter . . ."
> "Why is that?"
> "Because there's a new covenant. The prophet said so. Babies born into the new world and the new covenant will live. . . . He told all the bishops in his last message before we lost contact or whatever. Our babies are safe." (149)

This lack of fear for her own fate, or that of the potential child, possibly improves the chances of the mother and baby's survival, if there is any chance at all. The obstetrics field today often warns women, based on numerous studies, that there is a possible relationship between maternal stress and dangerous preterm births and low birth weight, a danger Jodi has clearly avoided with an insistently—and aggravatingly—positive attitude with regard to her situation. Dusty also finds out that Jodie has stolen prenatal vitamins and has taken them regularly, and has maintained a sufficiently nourishing diet. Thus, this conversation illustrates that if there was ever a possibility of a healthy pregnancy and birth at any point up to this one in the narrative, then Jodi's pregnancy would be it.

Further, the success of her birth would signal a renewal of the hierarchy of the settlement from which she escaped. She is a paradigm of this order, having embraced its Symbolic ideology, as Dusty is constantly reminded whenever she interacts with Jodi. Dusty asks,

> "What'd you do in your spare time in Huntsville?"
> "Canning and sewing and stuff. Like, taking care of everyone, making food, and fixing socks and stuff."
> "What do you like to do, though?"
> Jodi looked blank. (152)

These frustrating descriptions of Jodi's intellectual "absence" illuminate her embodiment of the "angel in the house" archetype, one who is "childlike, docile, submissive, the heroine of a life that *has no story*" (Gilbert and Gubar, 39, original emphasis). Later, Dusty admits to herself that "Jodi was a brat, but she'd been brought up in a rigid structure that only got more rigid after the plague. She would do what Dusty told her to because it was how she had always lived" (160). Jodi embodies and embraces the patriarchal ideal to an almost hyperbolic degree, which allows her to enclose her reason and acumen within a safe, hermetic system of convictions that withstands the challenges of the post-Apocalyptic world outside. Yet, those aspects of the dying population that have caused the Huntsville community to fall apart, a lack of acknowledgment of the impossibility of maintaining the Symbolic order amid the increasing disappearance of women, will eventually cause even Jodi to acknowledge the reality of what is happening around her. Jodi's seemingly impossible transformation from her delimited existence and "childlike" personality to one of a complex and independent maternal heroine reflects another facet of the transformation of the diegetic universe taking place post-catastrophe.

Before Jodi's transformation, she maintains the last vestige of hope for the preservation of patriarchal order through her irrational confidence in a successful pregnancy and parturition. The narrative further bolsters this hope with the fact that Jodi has safely escaped to Eden, to live in the protected "garden" of Dusty's relatively adamic homestead. The analogy of this new prospective genesis progresses as Jodi enters her seventh month of pregnancy and her fruit-like belly continues to grow, "rounder and bigger every day, hard as a pumpkin. . . . The child was alive, kicking . . . [Jodi's] appetite had increased. She got plenty of sleep. She was active and in fine spirits" (170). However, Dusty knows that these signs of flourishing maternity are illusory. Despite the promising signs of fruitful motherhood, Dusty

> did not want to hope. She tried to keep hope out of her, shutting all the doors and locking them with the keys of reason and evidence and precedent. Still, she could feel it seeping in, incorporeal and deathless, refusing to be refused. (170)

Thus, the impossible Eve and the Adam-midwife reside together in Eden, both of whom are fraudulent and spurious in their undermining of the archetypal biblical couple.

Honus, in the weeks before Jodi is due to give birth, returns. He has miraculously survived his travels to Colorado and back, and his surprising and unlikely arrival unsettles the atmosphere of the house that Jodi and Dusty now share. His appearance, both physical and figurative, changes the relative masculine and feminine dynamic between Dusty and Jodi. Dusty observes a "tall figure with broad shoulders walked through the door. He . . . revealed a handsome bearded face," describing features that Dusty herself has tried to mimic (172). When Honus addresses Dusty as "Brother," Jodi quickly reestablishes patriarchal law by "correcting" him: "She's not brother anybody. She's just Dusty. She pretended to be a man in Huntsville. Tell him, Dusty" (172). In this way, Jodi strips Dusty of domestic authority inherent in being the primary male, and attempts to realign the hierarchy of power in this small household: she is not a brother, but "just" Dusty—just a woman. Honus's reaction is visceral, and though he maintains his gratitude for Dusty's safeguard of Jodi, he is unable to grasp the distinction between Dusty's apparent biological sex and identity with her gendered masculine expression: "Honus looked her over, top to bottom. [Dusty] saw a mixture of confusion and disbelief cross his face. She thought she saw a little disgust as well" (172). Honus's sickened appraisal of the unfeminine woman stems from what Gilbert and Gubar call "sexual nausea," a side effect of "monster women" who are embodiments of the "male dread of women . . . the infantile dread of [their] autonomy" (34). This nausea also emerges from the Dusty's "unnatural" appearance, which has helped her survive the post-apocalyptic landscape, yet is an improvisation so dreadful that she seems not to have met any other woman who has attempted it, despite its potential efficacy as camouflage and defense against male predators. The coercive power of the patriarchal value of woman's feminine expression is so entrenched "in patriarchal culture [that] female speech and female 'presumption'—that is . . . revolt against male domination—are inextricably linked and inevitably daemonic" (Gilbert and Gubar, 35). Honus's disgust is another element of the last gasps of the judgment of patriarchal law, yet Dusty's masculine speech and revolt against a domination that is now a pre-apocalyptic archaism leads her to respond tersely and think: "'I'm safer as a man.' . . . *Damned if I need to explain myself to you . . . Asshole*" (173).

Over time, Dusty and Honus become lovers, and through this secretive coupling, which is motivated more by mutual desire than any profound idea of romance, Dusty compels Honus to transform his assumptions with regard to gender and same-sex relationships. Honus asks Dusty about her lost partner, Jack, and their pre-catastrophe sexual relationship. During her reminiscence, Dusty also mentions a number of her female sexual partners that she remembers fondly. Honus observes that "You've had a lot of partners . . . and I know some of them were women . . ." and Dusty reminds him that she is "from somewhere very different than you two" (213). Honus asks her,

> "Don't you want to know if I think it's gross?"
> "Not really." Old anger flared up.
> *What's the point, what's the point? Why fight about this now when it barely matters anymore?* (213, original italics)

The "old anger" has resurfaced, this familiar encounter with the pre-apocalyptic Symbolic and its sexual normativity. The Midwife's bisexuality and gender fluidity is as alien to the oblivious Mormon couple as if they had originated from different planets, yet it is this full-spectrum sexuality that has, in many ways, provided the Midwife the means to survive and rescue others, and it is the gender dogmatism and sexual insularity that has brought about the downfall of Jodi's and Honus's former community. However, over time, through conversations about pre-apocalyptic life, worries about Jodi's pregnancy, and even clinical discussions about sex, Honus's conservative doctrinal assumptions begin to weaken, as does the influence of the patriarchal Huntsville colony's religious order over his judgments.

Soon after this encounter between Dusty and Honus, Jodi goes into labor. After her initial contractions have begun, Honus secretly gives Dusty a gift he has carefully gleaned for her: a collection of books written by women that he has found during his forays to search for resources. This gift is remarkable, as it serves as a quiet acknowledgment of both the value of women's writing and the Midwife's place in this literary genealogy. Dusty is initially overcome by the profundity of the gift, but the small compendium causes Dusty to reflect on "how long it might be before there are new books published. And if any of them will be by women, ever again" (230). This reflection is, of course, particularly relevant in light of the narrator's own writing, who does not seem to see herself either taking part in the potential delivery of humanity's rebirth into a post-apocalypse, nor her part in the deliverance of literacy and writing, particularly as one among these women-authors. The fact that Dusty reflects on the future of writing at the same time that the fetus is descending Jodi's birth canal is no coincidence. Elison has formed the Midwife as a character whose writing is analogous to maternal labor. This moment is one of narrative self-reflection that underscores Dusty's lived chronicle as itself a conduit through which women's labor will reach parturition in human beings' tenuous future. She is not only midwife to humanity's future generation, but also deliverer of the future human memory and thus its literary archive. Dusty's reflection on the gift of women's writing echoes an anxiety centered in the preservation of the entirety of the human written archive, and her feverish contributions to her diary seem to illustrate Jacques Derrida's fateful words, that "the archive takes place at the place of originary and structural breakdown of the said memory" (*Archive Fever*, 11). The impetus to preserve memory by means of an archive, the printing of memory on some medium external to our cognition, is a compulsion that exists alongside the human drive to self-destruction, the Freudian "death drive." This act logically emerges in the post-apocalyptic landscape and impels the Midwife to function as *raconteuse*. Derrida suggests that this drive is the reason human beings are engrossed over the writing down of memory, since

> if there is no archive without consignation in an external place which assures the possibility of memorization, of repetition, of reproduction, or of reimpression, then we must also remember that repetition itself, the logic of repetition, indeed the repetition compulsion, remains, according to Freud, indissociable from the death drive. And thus from destruction. (12)

In other words, the "logic" of compulsively writing in her diary is portrayed as a critical practice, despite (or because of) Dusty's constant reminders that humanity and human beings will soon be extinguished. She writes: "*Each and every one of us=last person on Earth*" (234, original italics). This extinction leaves no one to read her diary entries, suggesting her continued documentation is driven by a compulsion to contribute to that which she feels most keenly disappearing—the archive of women's voices and memory—whether or not anyone will be left to read her legacy. Derrida, in an essay titled *"No Apocalypse, No Now"* (1984), examines the destructive capacity of a nuclear war, an argument that speaks to catastrophes such as a fatal plague, in that

> its being-for-the-first-time-and-perhaps-for-the-last-time, its absolute inventiveness . . . is obviously the possibility of an irreversible destruction, leaving no traces, of the juridico-literary archive—that is, total destruction of the basis of literature and criticism. Not necessarily the destruction of humanity, of the human habitat, nor even of other discourses (arts or sciences), nor even indeed of poetry or the epic; these latter might reconstitute their living process and their archive, at least to the extent that the structure of that archive (that of a nonliterary memory) implies, structurally, reference to a real referent external to the archive itself. (26)

Dusty's new world is distinct in the fact that the external archive remains preserved in printed matter strewn and scattered across the landscape despite the crumbling human populace. It is human beings who hold nonliterary memory and what Derrida calls "symbolic capacity" and *survivance*, the capacity that places the language of literature "at the very heart of life" ("Apocalypse," 28). Perhaps it is precisely the preservation of memories of the apocalyptic event in literature that prevents its non-diegetic realization. The novel's ultimate failure to catalyze catastrophe, a failure that Derrida refers to as *destinerrance*, is the central impetus and crisis of apocalyptic literature. Derrida states that this mode of writing conveys "the necessity and the impossibility of thinking the event, the coming . . . of a first time which would also be a last time. But the destinerrance of the sendings is precisely what both divides and repeats the first time and the last time alike," which centers the novel in a liminal zone of narrating its own demise while preventing it from occurring ("Apocalypse," 30). Is it possible that even if the unnamed Midwife cannot necessarily prevent the continued destruction of catastrophic plague, she may instead provide a means to prevent the widespread degradation of the maternal while simultaneously offering a means to preserve female voices? Dusty's observance of plague-induced stillbirths at the vanguard of the apocalyptic event is critical to capturing the narrative "destinerrance," and through diligent capture of her memories and experiences *in writing*, the Midwife performs the task of archivist in order to deliver the archive into the new world while delivering the prospective child that promises to embody the new generation.

During this critical moment in the narrative, the moments of parturition and the moments after, the novel centers exclusively on Dusty's first-person journal entries, providing an account of the tragedy in her own voice and reflecting the terror of what truly seems to entrench the Midwife's ultimate capitulation to humanity's doom. Jodi begins to give birth, and as the baby emerges it is immediately clear to Dusty that this child has not escaped the Plague:

> *Knew it would end this way. Fucking knew it . . . frozen ground, we can't even bury the body. They named it. No point in writing it down. No point in naming it . . . No point, no point.* (233, original italics)

In this entry the novel returns to the idea of the unnamed, which is indicative of that which is dying away. These extinctions include the function and necessity of midwives and the lost possibility of live human births—symbolized by the stillborn child. The stillbirth is a resounding proclamation that the hope and expectations of these three characters were misplaced and that human beings are really dying away. This is a realization so shattering that the narrative lens shifts quickly away from this scene. The story expands beyond Dusty's written lamentations to chronicles that are being written by the entirety of human survivors:

> Chronicles were written all over the world. Some were diaries, like the *Book of the Unnamed Midwife*. Others were histories of cities and settlements as the years moved by. Each marked time in their own way. Some were read. Others lay forgotten when their owners stopped writing. . . . The new year went largely unmarked except in these books. (Elison, 234)

The unexpected switch to this wider lens narratively amplifies the crisis of the stillbirth and the devastation experienced by Jodi, Dusty, and Honus. But it also links the chronicling of the apocalyptic plague and its aftermath to the criticality of the archive of writing as the means by which human beings will avert entire elimination with the final breath of the last human being. Thus, the Midwife contributes to a critical archival role in delivering the writing from one world to the next, echoing her deliverance of Jodi's baby in her written account.

However, the hope that she managed to cultivate during Jodi's pregnancy demonstrates that Dusty is capable of optimism with regard to the possibility of live birth. Yet, the novel takes another unusual turn, again widening the narrative lens and describing the circumstances of the remaining human beings in the rest of the world:

> If they could have compared notes, one colony of survivors to another, they would have found that the number of successful human births on Earth that year had been zero. But they did not know, and so hope persisted. (235)

The immense hope in the promise of Jodi's seemingly healthy pregnancy, coupled with the magnitude of the loss of the last hope for human regeneration is nearly unbearable for the Midwife. As Jodi refuses to eat and continues to decline in health, Dusty "thought Honus was right and Jodi would die, but it was such a small thing beside her dawning certainty that no children would ever be born again. *Never again, never again look upon this wasteland*" (236, original italics). The wasteland may be a reference to the decimation of humanity, but is likely also a metaphor for the wasteland of women's reproductive capacity, for which Jodi was a final hope. This seeming defeat leads to Dusty's determination to leave the house and continue her wandering journey.

Dusty embraces the relief of detachment by embodying vanishing motherhood as she and Honus make love: "He crawled into her lap with an urgency that woke everything in her. . . . He clung to her like a child, and she was mother and lover and barely sane" (236). Their copulation leads Honus to ask Dusty to be his second wife, asserting that "God sent Jodi to you for a reason" (239). Honus also mentions that Dusty may be pregnant, suggesting that the possibility may be reason enough for Dusty to remain with him and Jodi. Dusty is dismayed by this regression to chauvinism, and proceeds to

> show him her cache of pills and rings and patches. "This is my plan. This is what makes sense to me. Not dying while giving birth to a dead baby. I'm going to try and give them to your wife before I leave, because without someone to attend her, she might not get through this again. . . . [Y]our wife may be the only woman in the county or in the state after I leave. . . . [Y]ou'll have an accident so that someone else can marry her. . . . As long as you've got her, you've got *trouble*." (240, emphasis mine)

It is precisely this idea of Butlerian feminine "trouble" that Dusty herself evokes when Honus forgets his previous acknowledgment of Dusty's autonomy and self-reliance as well as the unavoidable tragedy of Jodi's stillbirth. Honus clings again to the pre-apocalyptic and patriarchal idea of possession and dominion over a woman with whom he has had sex and whom he may have impregnated. This idea of "trouble" is the focus of the first paragraphs of Butler's *Gender Trouble*, a term stemming from Jean-Paul Sartre, "for whom all desire, problematically presumed as heterosexual and masculine, was defined as *trouble*" (vii). Though Dusty's statement is pointed toward the potential trouble Jodi will cause, she is, in fact, referring to herself. As long as Honus "has" her, *Dusty*, he will have trouble, since Dusty persistently and firmly challenges his assumptions of patriarchy. As Butler states, women who push gender boundaries evince

> unanticipated agency, of a female "object" who inexplicably returns the glance, reverses the gaze, and contests the place and authority of the masculine position. The radical dependency of the masculine subject on the female "Other" suddenly exposes his autonomy as illusory. (vii)

Dusty fully embodies the destabilization, or "troubling," of gender, as a bisexual woman who expresses as masculine and conveys fervent and unfeigned pleasure during her sexual encounter with Honus. Honus offers to protect (possess) Dusty, and she rejects the idea (240). When Dusty insists that she will leave, Honus is overcome with emotion, asking

> "Can't you just . . ." Honus was not crying yet, but she could see it coming.
> *I can't and you can't. Jodi needs you and I don't. Get the hint, Honus.* (243, original italics)

Honus's masculine position, as articulated by Butler, is undermined by the Midwife who remains insistently queer. Dusty further exposes the "cultural performance" of being female and the "performative construction of an original and true sex," which is made manifest by her interactions with both Honus and Jodi (Butler, viii).

Jodi and Honus predictably return to Huntsville together, but they find that there are only a dozen inhabitants left, and the remaining men are committing suicide one by one. However, the most painful atrocity that they witness is Bishop Lewis's forced marriage and nightly rape of young Patty. Jodi and Honus decide to leave Huntsville for good and return to the house they had once shared with Dusty, and finally only Lewis and Patty remain in the settlement. After the move, Jodi embraces the maternal anger Marianne Hirsch describes, which initiates her transition to the heroic maternal that is characteristic of the new emerging post-apocalyptic protagonist. This maternal turn occurs when Jodi eschews all of her patriarchal values and decides to go back to Huntsville and rescue Patty. And it is Jodi who ends up taking the gun from Honus and shooting Lewis herself when Honus is unable to execute the madman and rapist. Jodi also abnegates the Marian ideal that she has uncritically embodied her entire life. Jodi comforts Honus as he remains in shock after witnessing Lewis die in front of him. When Jodi eventually dies due to another pregnancy, it is Patty who burns the body while Honus remains "wrecked with grief" (254). These two remaining survivors, Patty (who is "barren") and Honus, end up living together in isolation until their deaths.

Thus, through her experiences at the settlement, Dusty witnesses the last vestiges of patriarchal law, the evolution of pre- to post-apocalyptic mother, and the collapse of the final community functioning within the Symbolic.

MATRIARCHAL LAW AND A NEW HIVE MENTALITY

During the period in which Honus resides with Jodi and Dusty, Dusty discovers the diary that Honus has kept during his "missionary" trip. Honus is required by his religious order to maintain a log of his travels, and both his entries and those of the Midwife are carefully preserved and labeled by the future scribes who preserve these writings. Honus traveled with a partner named Langdon, and these two members of the Mormon colony witness gruesome horrors as they search for the mythical "temple in Denver," seeing numerous corpses of those killed by the Plague or by each other (179). But the most horrific of their experiences on the road is centered in what the future scribes have labeled "the First Hive" (206). The name comes from a new community arrangement organized by a woman survivor named Amanda. Honus states in this diary that

> we've been with Amanda in her hive, as she calls it, for two days. They caught us that night on the roof and brought us here . . . I was stripped nude and force-fed more alcohol . . . Amanda is a tall beautiful girl. . . . She wears clothing that barely exists. . . . She doesn't speak to us. She speaks to all the men as though they were one person. There are twenty men here. (206)

Honus goes on to describe a room with no windows and several performance stages, and little need for sustenance since the inhabitants largely drink alcohol and consume psychotic substances. Honus's attempts to escape cause "a group of the men to stop me. They were making this terrible noise. I'm terrified" (207). Honus is thus captured in a manner that echoes Shawna's abduction early in the narrative.

This "hive," dominated by the unenslaved (and even joyful) Amanda as its queen, is a burgeoning feminocentric new society. Although Langdon chooses to embrace this way of life, Honus is mortified. When Amanda calls Honus in to speak with her alone, he states that "she made me kneel in front of her as she lay naked . . . I tried not to look, but it was such a trial . . . I fought temptation, I struggled like Jacob" (207). Honus desperately grasps onto his belief that his wife, Jodi, still lives and waits for him, but he simultaneously cannot condone what he is witnessing, writing that "I couldn't believe this freaking abomination was really happening" (208). The portrayal of this new form of community follows a literary convention of portraying matriarchal societies as insect- or ant-like communities. Graham J. Murphy, in his essay "Considering Her Ways: In(ter)secting Matriarchal Utopias" (2008), traces this analogy from Charlotte Perkins Gilman's *Herland* (1915) to Stephen Baxter's *Coalescent* (2004). Murphy states that "matriarchal Utopias likened (chiefly by patriarchal visitors) to hives or anthills or colonies are common to all . . . of these texts" (272). Amanda perpetuates this concept when telling Honus "she was the queen of the hive and she needed more drones to bring her honey" (207). This odd manner of seduction overturns the conventional patriarchal roles between men and women, as Amanda invites the "men all [to] succumb to arthropodal coding, divested of power and reduced to pseudo-drones servicing the needs of the hive" (Murphy, 273). And yet the males in the narrative, starving and bereft on many fronts—for sex, food, shelter—happily accede to Amanda's proposition in a community protected both from the devastation outside and from patriarchal norms within. Honus notes that the men "were all drinking alcohol or taking drugs. It seemed like that was what they did all day. Some of them were dancing on the stages. . . . Some of them were having sex with one another" (208). In opposition to the fights for resources and the victimization resulting from gender expression that Dusty has witnessed, Amanda has facilitated a means for all of the men in her hive to no longer feel hunger or inhibition, and have their sexual needs satisfied without violent competition or exploitation. No one must perform masculinity for protection, and no one is compelled to threaten mortal violence in order to acquire resources. Langdon seems to accept this arrangement, or at least succumbs to his assimilation into it, eschewing the patriarchal values that Honus continues to desperately grasp. Honus has described his companion as suffering to the point of appearing suicidal, and Amanda's embrace of Langdon without prerequisite or violence illustrates that the hive functions within the sphere of what Murphy refers to as a matriarchal utopia, illustrating that "the males' social function within the broader hive matriarchy is resoundingly nonpatriarchal and resolutely queer in its complete overhaul of the power that typically accompanies masculinist gender coding. Willingly or not, they all eventually serve the matriarchal hive" (Murphy, 273). Honus, who is initially the paradigm of masculinist gender coding, finds that his ideology is being decimated in the presence of the hive structure, since the hive provides for the human needs that cannot be fulfilled post-catastrophe through patriarchal social codes. Honus manages to escape before he also succumbs, finally returning to his pregnant wife, Jodi.

The hive structure exhibits the "monstrosity" that is evinced by the uninhibited women that Honus encounters in the post-catastrophe new world. Honus's perspective is one of phallocentric heteronormativity, which is a lens that allows the narrative to illustrate the distinction between the pre-apocalyptic Symbolic "gender codes" and the monstrous post-human process of "becoming insect." In other words, the "men in these stories are typically unable to accept becoming-insect with its multiplicities, metamorphoses, and alternative figurations of 'woman' that redefine (and ultimately discard) modernity's heteronormative and phallocentric codes" (Murphy, 274). Honus cannot accept the hive structure that is centered on a female queen, yet maintains his acceptance of the phallocentric abusive structure of the colony that sent him, and Langdon, to their demise. Honus never truly understands or accepts the Midwife's gender expression and lack of quiescence "proper" to a woman's role as she, like the hive queens, "holds no stock in heteronormative codes or romantic idealization" (Murphy, 273). He witnesses, due to the absence of maternal possibility and nonexistent patriarchal domination, a new queer and gender-fluid community of post-humanity that clashes entirely with his cognizance of the Symbolic.

Beyond serving as a means to provide solace for its members, the hive forms a family structure in a world where women can no longer have children. Thus, as the narrative progresses, the matriarchal hive structure begins to emerge as the most viable means of not only survival but communal intimacy. In a return to the frame story, centered in the distant future, the young scribes set to work preserving an account of the Midwife's own observations of a matriarchal hive. Similar to the experience of Honus and Langdon, the Midwife senses the proximity of the hive before actually seeing its members, lending the community an air of what Murphy refers to as "infrahuman," or "the long-standing intimacies of 'human' and 'animal' suggest[ing] that any ontological separation between them is fractious, perhaps even illusory" (266). This ambiance, emphasized through the members' wearing of furs and absence of sexual inhibitions, also underscores its alterity. The Midwife describes the matriarchal hierarchy of the community in her diary entry:

> Vivian and fourteen men. . . . Not one of them made a move without her say. Never seen anything like it. . . . Invited me to dinner and a long group fuck. Didn't join but watched. Amazing. Laughing the whole time. She got off more times than I can count, gave them almost nothing. Threw them out if they came too fast or couldn't take direction. (257)

Appropriate behaviors are established by the "(brood)mother . . . Social roles are not enforced according to heteronormative ideals but according to strict internal regulation that services the needs of the community" (Murphy, 269). The Hives of Vivian and Amanda eschew all pre-apocalyptic normativity centered in male-dominant hierarchies and presents radical alterity amid the detritus of the Symbolic order. These are not the only hives described in the narrative, but the hive is also not the final form that community that will take in the new world. It is through future evolutionary iterations of nonpatriarchal community that will finally lead to the birth of a living baby.

BIRTH IN THE POST-APOCALYPTIC ÆTHER

At one point during the Midwife's travels, two inhabitants of a community called Fort Nowhere encounter her by accident. They happen to discover each other during a vulnerable moment, when the Midwife has let down her masculine guise. One of the two inhabitants is a woman, and she peaceably invites the Midwife to visit their community that is "enclosed. Defensible . . . we never turn down women or girls" (263). To gain the Midwife's trust, Ava describes her ordeal of being sold to "gangs of guys," and reveals that the "first gang killed my daughter. She was thirteen" (263). Ava has avoided further pregnancies due to her pre-catastrophe implanted Intra-Uterine Device, and in sharing her pain of maternal loss, the two women exchange a form of maternal intuition, and thus "they shared a moment, a knowing," an understanding that only female characters can share, and Dino, Ava's male companion, "did not intrude" (264). This mutual understanding centered in maternity is one that drives a number of studies of motherhood theory. Shannon K. Carter, in her essay "Gender and Childbearing Experiences" (2009), deconstructs this intuitive sense through Karl Marx's argument that human "essence" is fulfilled through work, and as such "gender differences in relationships to reproduction result in a different reproductive consciousness for women and men. For women, connection and integration with the rest of the human species are reaffirmed through the labor involved in reproduction" (123). This generalization may border on being reductive with regard to maternal experiences, but nonetheless underscores the reality that the maternal characters in all of the novels in this monograph share. There is an inescapable "reproductive consciousness" that is especially apparent for the women who still possess memories of a world in which motherhood was possible. The fact that the Midwife has never, and will never give birth does not excise her from this consciousness, as

> the fact that some women do not reproduce does not change the gendered social relations of childbearing or the resulting gendered reproductive consciousness. Even though all women do not participate in the acts of being pregnant and giving birth, it is only women and not men who can. (Carter, 124)

This results in a *collective* reproductive consciousness among maternal characters that becomes central to the final scenes of the novel despite the fact that women continue to die in pregnancy or during birth, and stillbirths are the closest that women come to becoming mothers.

Thus, the Midwife agrees to join Ava and Dino and finally reaches her ultimate stop, the settlement called Fort Nowhere. While there, the Midwife, who adopts her final moniker "Jane," decides to expand her crucial diary to include the entries and experiences of other inhabitants of the community. This section of the journal is labeled "The Book of Histories and Hives" by the future scribes, and includes accounts of a multiplicity of matriarchal hives that had begun to flourish across the population of survivors in this post-apocalypse context (271). Despite the fact that the hives satisfy numerous necessities for their members, these matriarchal utopias are not panaceæ for all unfulfilled social needs. For example, one of the diary entries written by an inhabitant of Fort Nowhere, Andrea, recalls her encounter with the hive of Kacie, and states that Kacie

> tried to teach me how to keep a few guys on a string, to protect me and take care of me. Kacie had five guys. . . . People here at the fort call it a hive. Kacie said it was just the natural reaction to things . . . I could never get used to it. (273)

Andrea had decided to leave the protection of the hive and, like Shawna, is captured by a band of men and "raped for days," eventually escaping impregnated (274). Jane has warned Andrea of the repercussions of her pregnancy, and Andrea states "I'll take anything after the baby dies. If I make it . . . I don't care if none of the babies live. We don't deserve it, as a species" (274). In this entry, Andrea reveals an ambivalence with regard to the maternal, a rejection of the reproductive consciousness that may have been mitigated by forming a matriarchal hive of her own. Yet, impregnation of the hive queen would have likely led to her death and bereavement of the surviving hive members. Andrea's experience reveals the fracturing of her connection with the new gender hierarchy that is burgeoning in Fort Nowhere, and as a result she cannot imagine the future absent the patriarchal Symbolic that has exploited and silenced her. Unsurprisingly, despite the fact that most women now demonstrate the possibility of surviving their pregnancies and deliveries, "Andrea died a week after birth" (279).

The subsistence of matriarchal hives, as is true in the insect world from which this concept is taken, critically depends on the survival of its "queen"—a significant shortcoming in a world where pregnancy is almost necessarily followed by the queen's death. The hive also falls short in providing another need: a sense of emotional connection. In a journal entry written by Barry, the absence of emotional connection is intimately tied to the absence of the possibility of motherhood:

> I saw my first hive. This woman was very smart. She looked at me like she was a spider and I was a fly, but she was calling herself Queen B. . . . We would

work all day and pretty much fuck all night . . . I would do it again, if someone started a hive here. . . . But I really wanted something more. . . . [Queen Bonnie] said she had her tubes tied. There wasn't a future there. (275)

Despite the fact that Barry's needs are largely fulfilled in the hive, he seeks intimacy with someone who could be his child's mother, and the absence of this possibility, as fatal as it would be for the prospective mother, serves as the ultimate motivation for Barry to leave the hive and seek some form of kinship that now may exist at Fort Nowhere. Other written accounts describe inabilities to come to terms with the queer community and the absence of heteronormative monogamy in the hive. Yet, these complaints are largely those of the male characters who seem unable to come to terms with the new post-apocalyptic social structure that grows increasingly matriarchal as the narrative reaches its conclusion. One of the most fascinating entries provides insight into the impending social order, and is centered on unwritten chronicles emerging from another part of the world: "England and Ireland were covered with hives. Slavers were killed in public when they were caught. . . . A small army of women ranged across Wales . . . led by a woman who called herself Buddug" (Elison, 282). The (re)appearance of Queen Boudicca alludes to a significant historical moment in Western (and human) history, one that recalls a transition from a population that welcomed warrior queens to one that was overtaken by the Roman patriarchal hierarchy. Buddug is "resurrected" to re-instantiate a matriarchal society that returns this population of survivors to its pre-Roman state.[2,3]

Jane maintains her own journal entries while residing at Fort Nowhere, recording the names of the dead prospective mothers in her chronicle. She also tracks a remarkable series of stillbirths, all named "Nobody": "not nameless . . . But they are dreamless. Don't suffer, don't toil . . . Nobody, child of Shawna . . . Nobody Obermeyer, son of Jodi and Honus Obermeyer . . . Gwen, daughter of Andrea. Gang-raped by slavers. Put them down. Andrea died a week after the birth. . . . Nobody, daughter of that girl who never spoke. Showed up pregnant. . . . Maternal death is better this year, getting better all the time. Not a selling point" (279). The list continues to grow, and Jane remains at Fort Nowhere for fifteen years as "the earth grew quiet, and everything seemed to team with life and hold its breath, waiting" (282). This period of waiting reaches its conclusion when Jane takes on an apprentice, Shayla, who begins her education with the pregnant woman Colleen. On the day that Colleen goes into labor, Jane and Shayla prepare to deliver another stillbirth, or perhaps a live baby that will not survive long. The baby drops into Jane's hands, and "Jane wrapped the still-crying baby in a towel. She didn't look the child in the face . . . [and] Colleen prepared to nurse the child" (286). Strangely, the baby continues to breathe: "Jane thought she counted six hours since this baby was born. This was longer than any baby had lasted so far" (287). And thus Colleen's baby, Rhea, becomes the first birth of a child that survives birth and goes on to thrive. The final lines of the novel state that the "population picked up, slowly . . . . But there were children in the world. One by one, they were lost and found" (288). These final lines can be rewritten to state that "there were mothers in the world. One by one, *they* were lost and found." The absence of mothers had led to a population in hopeless decline, but a re-framing of social life that rejects patriarchal norms has led to the conditions that allow for maternity to re-emerge and predominate.

What are the implications, then, of the reemergence of the maternal? The novel's closing frame narrative, the Epilogue, makes this immediately clear in its opening line: "Mother Ina untied her belly and hung it on the peg . . . Ina lived in the House of Mothers because she had survived the birth of a living child" (289). Ina is the "eminently pregnant" character from the narrative's opening frame, who led the young male scribes in the copying of the Midwife's journal. In the closing of the frame narrative of the novel, the narrative has returned to the distant future several generations after Rhea's birth. Surviving mothers are heralded as authority figures, and midwives are bestowed with social distinction. Women lead bands of warriors who continue to search the world outside for other females. This is a world entirely unlike the one into which the Midwife first awoke. The narrative never includes mention of the unnamed Midwife's own mother, a woman who resides on the other side of apocalyptic catastrophe. Her absence underscores the Midwife's position as untethered to the new maternal order. As an untethered, unnamed, and un-gendered character, the Midwife is positioned to assist in delivering a new maternal world, one that leads to generations of daughters, mothers and matriarchs who overturn assumptions about them that had once seemed inescapable.

NOTES

1. See Exodus 1:15-21 in the *New American Standard Bible*.
2. This new society is one that develops in this novel's sequel.
3. This new society is one that Elison explores in her novel's sequel, *The Book of Etta* (2017).

Chapter 3

NEW MOTHER

To Resist and Dis-Obeah in the Wasted Inner City of Brown Girl in the Ring *(1999)*

In his essay "Epistemic Disobedience, Independent Thought, and De-colonial Freedom" (2009), Walter Mignolo describes the "epistemic privilege of the First World," in which

> the First World had indeed the *privilege of inventing the classification and being part of it.* As a consequence, the impression that knowledge-making has no geo-political location and that its location is in an ethereal place . . . has been successfully naturalized. (8)

This epistemic privilege has led to a general assumption of knowledge generation as driven by and generated by the West without the consideration of or contribution from the "global South." Epistemic privilege, like the privilege that accompanies males with white skin in daily life, is taken for granted and unquestioned, and permeates all forms of generative knowledge, including literary genres such as post-apocalyptic narratives. For this reason, a white male savior for humanity in a post-catastrophe setting has been taken for granted throughout the existence of dystopian fiction, and the absence of women of color as protagonists in these narratives has remained unquestioned until recent decades. The two previous chapters of this book have argued for the re-imagining of the event of human birth amid devastation and the capabilities of gravid female characters as protagonists in their post-apocalyptic universes. The concept, however, of a black female narrative protagonist with a young child in her arms whose actions save humanity from degradation is one that is almost unimaginable. However, this chapter explores a novel that invites us to consider what might happen if submerged or suppressed stories and voices of mothers of color carrying children and reject victimization were normalized, and whose agency brings about the creation of a radically different world. Nalo Hopkinson's Locus Award-winning novel, *Brown Girl in the Ring* (1999), falls within a change that Mignolo traces to the present day. "History," he says, "is globally moving toward a polycentric world . . . calling for an 'epistemic awakening' of Africans and Third World scholars and intellectuals that had already been happening and continues to grow around the world" (10).

In the earliest of the novels I examine, *Brown Girl in the Ring* (1999), the protagonist is remarkable for undermining the assumptions of a woman caring for a child. But the protagonist and the narrative itself is also an exceptional example of what Reynaldo Anderson refers to as one of "the seeds for a Black speculative movement challenging white racist normativity and Black parochialism . . . sown by creative intellectuals" (230). The novel is highly influenced by mythology emerging from author Nalo Hopkinson's diasporic African culture in the Caribbean. As Hopkinson states in a 2003 interview, she seeks

> to imagine how Caribbean culture might metonymize technological progress if it was in our hands: in other words, what stories we'd tell ourselves about our technology—what our paradigms for it might be. The current metaphors for technology and social behaviors and systems are largely from Graeco-Roman mythology. We call our spaceships Apollo and our complexes Oedipus. We talk about cyberspace. So I wondered what metaphors we (Caribbean people) would create for technologies that we had made, how we would think about those technologies . . . [such as t]he operating system, which governs a building, is called an eshu, who is a West African deity who can go everywhere, see everything. (150)

Hopkinson re-imagines a post-apocalyptic novel by reinventing the Greco-Roman literary genealogy, and conceiving this landscape through the eyes not of a conventional Byronic-hero woman or man, solemnly making their way through a devastated landscape. Instead, Hopkinson upends assumptions with regard to heroism by adopting a non-Western perspective in the formation of a maternal protagonist.

This chapter will argue that it is precisely the non-Western, unorthodox African-diasporic elements of *Brown Girl in the Ring* that contribute to the protagonist's ability to seek out the narrative's exploitative and powerful putative *übermensch* and change the direction of her post-apocalyptic world. This non-Western Anglophone narrative direction is reflected also in the Caribbean dialect of the characters' speech. Within the Caribbean diaspora, the characters exhibit a multiplicity of voices, as Carol B. Duncan notes, explaining that Ti-Jeanne

> is the mother of an unnamed infant baby boy and the reluctant heir to a spiritual legacy passed on from her grandmother, Gros-Jeanne. Weaving elements from

> Yoruban orisha, Haitian *vodun* and Jamaican *pocomania* together, Hopkinson creates a Caribbean diasporic religion uniquely responsive to the life situations of migratory Caribbean peoples in Toronto. (170)

Further, by coming to grips with her supernatural abilities passed on to her through her Caribbean heritage, Ti-Jeanne takes back the magical abilities stolen from the women in her family and frees her mother from bondage in which she is being held. By ultimately embracing her African cultural heritage, Ti-Jeanne joins the lineage of mothers into which she was born to overturn stereotypes and save her world as one of the most conventionally oppressed subjects in intersectional literary heroism—a black single mother.

In the novel *Brown Girl in the Ring*, the protagonist inhabits a post-apocalyptic urban setting in the heart of Toronto, Canada. Sherbourne, or "The Burn," is an insular community where the conventional societal rules do not apply because the neighborhood is largely abandoned by the government and the elite. The protagonist, Ti-Jeanne, is being haunted by frightening visions that are driven by extraordinary powers engendered by her Afro-Caribbean maternal heritage. Ti-Jeanne must learn to control her powers with the instruction of her grandmother while rejecting the external presumptions imposed on her as a mother. As the narrative progresses, we find out that her child's father works for a mobster-like character named Rudy who exhibits superhuman abilities, a power, we learn, that he must forcefully appropriate from mostly female victims by robbing them of their souls and sovereignty.

Throughout the novel, we see Ti-Jeanne come to grips with an inherent supernatural ability that she has struggled against but ultimately embraces. She reaches this level of maturation and acceptance despite the fact that her own mother lost her mind and abandoned her. Near the end of the novel, Ti-Jeanne must combat the monstrous Rudy face-to-face. However, she finds out that Rudy is, in fact, her own grandfather, and Rudy maintains his power, in part, by magically imprisoning the spirit of his own daughter, Ti-Jeanne's mother. Ti-Jeanne's mother, Mi-Jeanne, is trapped and enslaved by her father, a man who means to maintain his paternal grip on these generations of women by seizing what was formerly only women's magical power—witchcraft—and by means of possessing these women's agency—their souls. Rudy states, more than once, that "the women in that family been giving me trouble from so long" (172). We see that Mi-Jeanne has lost this battle of sovereignty against her father (and the patriarchal order he represents), but she maintains some degree of independent thought, enough to defy Rudy and warn Ti-Jeanne that Rudy has sent his own daughter, Mi-Jeanne, to kill her own daughter. When she fails in this attempted homicide, Tony, Ti-Jeanne's lover and the father of her child, will attempt to carry out the murder instead.

There is no mistaking the conflict between the mother and father figures, the fight of motherhood against oppression and possession by fathers. This fight for autonomy is driven by the fact that these mothers, *Obeah*-women, are seen by other characters as witches, and as such carry with them the stigma of being supernaturally threatening to the narrative's precarious Symbolic order. These women embody the threat that has driven witch trials throughout human history, in cultures around the world (including the Afro-Caribbean tradition that is so formative for this novel).

INTERSECTIONAL SINGLE MOTHERHOOD

Post-apocalyptic narratives speak to the social ills of the culture from which they emerge, and in dystopian narratives centered on maternal protagonists, we see this metaphoric critique consistently re-emerge. The violence and oppression of women persists in our present moment, and this is especially true for single mothers of color who are drawing attention to systemic oppression through their activism. In their formative book *Intersectionality* (2018), Patricia Hill Collins and Sirma Bilge state that

> drawing on cultural ties to the African diaspora, black women activists also saw their roles as mothers and othermothers as important for political action. . . . Their images were maligned in popular culture. They were disproportionately targets of violence against women. They were mothers who lacked the means to care for their children as they would have liked, but had ties to the value placed on mothering across the African diaspora. (24)

The culture surrounding maternity within the African diaspora has scaffolded women in care of children, bringing about a reconception of the way black women see themselves in terms of motherhood with regard to activism on behalf of themselves, other women, or the diaspora as a whole. For this reason, in part, the visibility of black mothers in fictional narratives is critical, particularly in post-apocalyptic novels, in order to bring about a new vision of the future for black women in the midst of societal devastation.

In her essay on the ways in which fiction tells the stories of women of color who suffer from abuse, Silvia Martínez-Falquina states that

> the authors' engagement in a dialogue with the past also evidences how the tentacles of sexism and racism function in unison and are deeply rooted in even the most reputedly democratic socio-cultural structures of today. . . . Both the voicing of specifically African American and Native American vindications and their dialogue with global feminist developments point to a productive

relationship of text and context which responds to the activist impulse to make a difference in the world through writing. (119)

Though Hopkinson often demurs from stating that her work is intended to make an activist or socio-critical statement, her novel—a narrative that is so exceptional and unprecedented—cannot escape from having a significant impact on the direction and possibilities of post-apocalyptic writing by drawing a black mother and her child into the role of heroism.

Throughout the narrative the protagonist, Ti-Jeanne, must calm her infant's cries, find care for him though she puts her life at risk, and even enter into dangerous situations while breastfeeding. This attention to the incessant and consuming needs of an infant entirely upends the image of the "maternal" that Judith Butler states is characteristic of the Symbolic. Yet, the challenge of confronting oppression while carrying and caring for a child is a situation in which many single mothers—especially black single mothers—find themselves daily. The fact that Nalo Hopkinson has overturned the typically patriarchally driven post-apocalyptic narrative by burdening her protagonist with a suckling child not only shatters the "glass ceiling" of what is possible in these narratives, but also speaks to the reality of working-class single mothers for whom a shattered landscape is a daily experience.

In the second paragraph of the novel's first chapter, the protagonist is introduced with her child in her arms:

> Rocking along in the back of a pedicab, she held Baby, cradling her child's tiny head in one hand to cushion it from the jolting. . . . Baby was trying to find his mouth with his thumb. Ti-Jeanne took his hand away long enough to ease the little blue mitten onto his fist. (9)

This quiet and intimate moment between mother and infant sets the stage for a narrative that often returns to the protagonist's maternal care. The pedicab driver, after dropping off Ti-Jeanne and her child, "moved off quickly, not even looking around for more customers. *Coward*, Ti-Jeanne thought to herself" (10). The cab driver hurries to escape the dangerous neighborhood in which he has dropped off mother and child. The protagonist lives in a neighborhood that has been abandoned after an apocalyptic event has led to an economic collapse, a collapse so severe that it is called, in the media, "The Doughnut Hole." "That's what they call it when an inner city collapses and people run to the suburbs," says Mr. Reed, the "self-appointed town librarian" (10–11). Nevertheless, the world will not wait for Ti-Jeanne to finish raising her child. She must care for the infant while traversing the hardship of a devastated inner city.

In an often-utilized literary motif, the effects of the apocalyptic event are revealed through media sources in the narrative, in this case through news headlines posted on a community bulletin board:

> Crime at all-time high but budget cuts force ontario provincial police to downsize . . . Toronto city hall moves to suburbs: safer for our employees, says mayor . . . Riot cops lay down arms, army called in: toronto is "war zone," says head of police union. (11)

These headlines reveal that those in Ti-Jeanne's milieu must fend for themselves as they will not have police protection and will not have access to jobs and other resources as business interests abandon the area. For this reason, residents of "the Burn" must depend on each other for all of their resources and needs, and barter for these necessities. Ti-Jeanne lives with her grandmother, Gros-Jeanne, who educates her in traditional methods of healing. Gros-Jeanne also attempts to teach Ti-Jeanne the Old Ways based in worship of the spirits, but Ti-Jeanne resists this education, despite the visions that the deities compel her to see.

At one point in the narrative, all three generations of mothers are reunited when Mi-Jeanne, so far referred to as "Crazy Betty," returns to her mother's home where Ti-Jeanne is also staying. Mi-Jeanne is blind, and her body is without reason or cognitive ability since Rudy has captured her spirit to serve him as a "calabash duppy." Ti-Jeanne is shocked to learn that this strange woman is her own mother, and Gros-Jeanne is ecstatic to have her daughter returned. And with this new reunion, Mi-Jeanne meets her grandchild:

> Mami Gros-Jeanne sat down beside her daughter. "Mi-Jeanne, you know you have a grandchild? A boy, Mi-Jeanne!" She took Mi-Jeanne's hand and led it to Baby's face, holding on tightly in case her mad daughter tried to hurt the child. Instead Mi-Jeanne's face went soft and gentle as she felt the baby's face. (145)

There is an instinctual maternal care that is based in motherhood experience, and perhaps because of their experience in the obeah culture:

> Ti-Jeanne put Baby into her mother's arms . . . Mi-Jeanne's cracked, trembling hands moved automatically to support Baby's head and his back. She had been, after all, a mother. Mami watched the two women cradling the baby. . . . Her granddaughter was learning, learning how to reach out a healing hand to others, despite her own cares. She would make a good seer woman. (147)

Unfortunately, Mi-Jeanne missed this opportunity, as she turned her back on her mother, Gros-Jeanne, when Gros-Jeanne rejected Rudy. Mi-Jeanne sought out her father, who then exploited her spirit as a duppy for his own purposes: to rejuvenate his youth, to carry out criminal activities, and to gain revenge on Gros-Jeanne and the spirits who, he felt, rejected him.

The reunion of the three generations of mothers is short-lived, as Tony appears at the door with the purpose of murdering Gros-Jeanne at Rudy's bidding. Mi-Jeanne, in her duppy form, is compelled to oversee the murder of her own mother, making sure Tony carries it out and retrieves the heart to seal the deal that Rudy made with Premier Uttley. Gros-Jeanne is able to detect Mi-Jeanne's liminality, to some degree:

> Mami felt something change in the air around them . . . a misty redness that seemed to centre around Mi-Jeanne. Used to seeing into the spirit world, Mami briefly glimpsed something that might have been eyes burning with longing and loss, clutching hands. The mistiness faded, seeming to melt into Mi-Jeanne's flesh. (148)

Mi-Jeanne is fighting to remain in her human body, but as a being divided into flesh and duppy, or spirit, Mi-Jeanne is compelled to carry out Rudy's orders. Rudy feeds the cursed woman human flesh and blood to keep her dependent and subservient to him, forcing her to cannibalize and murder despite her longing to remain human and care for her daughter and grandchild. This conflict of maternal versus the monstrous is futile, and when Mi-Jeanne returns to the form of the duppy, the narrative changes her pronoun from "she" to "it," drawing a distinction between the once-human being and the disembodied murderous spirit: "*It* hated the man who kept *it* bound, neither alive nor dead. Rudolph Sheldon. One day *it*s chance would come, and then, Rudolph Sheldon, then. But for now, *it* was compelled to do Rudy's bidding" (156, emphasis added). Although the being is an "it," the duppy clearly has some willpower, as it/she seeks an opportunity to free itself from Rudy's grip. Until then, Mi-Jeanne, as a duppy, must oversee Tony's killing not just of Gros-Jeanne, but of Ti-Jeanne, completing Rudy's destruction of these three generations of mothers with the power he has taken from them.

Ti-Jeanne's heroic maternal journey truly begins once Gros-Jeanne is murdered by Tony and Ti-Jeanne discovers her body. Ti-Jeanne tries to fight to keep the "Vultures," the "Angels of Mercy" agents who work for Angel of Mercy Hospital from taking Gros-Jeanne's corpse in their collection of "biomaterial"—or body parts harvested for the use of the elite. Ti-Jeanne faints as she tries to chase the Vultures' ambulance and later wakes up because "it was her aching, milk-swollen breasts that finally brought Ti-Jeanne to herself as she knelt in the middle of the road. Baby was still back at the house. He would be hungry. He would need to be changed" (159). It is her maternal impulse that brings Ti-Jeanne back to consciousness and to the present, and reminds her of her commitment to continue her care for her young child. This impulse also drives her to face her fears, which would be insurmountable without the motivation provided by her unceasing concern for Baby. She sarcastically lists the demands being made on her:

> "Mami want me to turn bush doctor; Tony want me to dead; you want me to save your wicked soul . . ." She heard Baby's thin, hungry cry from the other bedroom. Her milk let down at the sound, dampening the front of her shirt. "God, not now, child. You ain't see I busy?" Busy. Ti-Jeanne almost laughed at the inadequacy of the word. (162)

Ti-Jeanne is suddenly confronted with her tasks: to newly embrace the old ways so that she can stop Tony and free her mother, but all while continuing to care for a dependent infant: "'La Diablesse. Soucouyant,' Ti-Jeanne muttered. This was her nightmare. Her own mother. And it was up to her to stop Mi-Jeanne" (164). In order to stop, or even just delay Mi-Jeanne from her homicidal task, she tells it to take her to Rudy:

> "Take we to Rudy place." Tony grabbed her wrist . . . "Woman, like you mad, or what?" . . . "I mad . . . ," Ti-Jeanne said. " . . . I mad at all of allyou for making me run around trying to save allyou, but allyou just digging yourselves in deeper . . ." "But Ti-Jeanne," Tony protested, . . . "you can't go to Rudy's. He'll just kill you . . . " "I tell you, I going . . . Mummy," Ti-Jeanne addressed [the duppy], "let me just go get the baby. He hungry. I could feed he while we walk." The fireball moved out of the way . . . Ti-Jeanne went into her own room to get Baby; Tony and the fireball followed her as if attached to her apron strings. She stared down at her child in his crib. Leave him here alone, perhaps to starve to death, or take him with them? Baby looked at her, reached for her. Another life tied to her apron strings. She picked him up, put him into his Snugli, and slung it onto her body. (165–166)

Ti-Jeanne has little choice. If she wants to save the life of her child and free her mother, she must carry and feed her baby while walking to face and battle the one she fears most: Rudy. This critical scene illustrates the decision that compels Ti-Jeanne into the role of the maternal heroine in the post-apocalypse: should she abandon her child, where perhaps he may survive, or take him with her, where he will be endangered by the conflict that Ti-Jeanne must face? Either choice will lead to endangering her child, which is a point that the author is making: Black single mothers are often faced with impossible choices with regard to their child's welfare, as Jennifer Nash argues in her essay "The Political Life of Black Motherhood": "black motherhood as both a site constituted by grief and expected loss and as a political position made visible (only) because of its proximity to death" (700). Although Hopkinson has stated in interviews that she is not making a political statement with her novel, her depiction of Ti-Jeanne's dispassionate yet devastating choice is an echo of black single mothers today: save her family by destroying it, or destroy her family by saving it? In this way, black motherhood is a form of post-apocalypse in itself.

The character of a black single mother as a heroine for the post-apocalyptic world is rife with complexities, as the literary depiction of black mothers carries substantial political significance. As Zakiyyah Iman Jackson states, in *Becoming Human: Matter and Meaning in an Antiblack World* (2020),

> the black mater(nal) marks the discursive-material trace effects and foreclosures of the dialectics of hegemonic common sense and that the anxieties stimulated by related signifiers, such as the black(ened) maternal image, voice, and life-world, allude to the latent symbolic-material capacities of black mater, as mater, as matter, to destabilize or even rupture the reigning order of representation that grounds the thought-world relation. (116)

Ti-Jeanne, her body, and her choices as a black mother form an intersection that complicates the idea of the post-apocalyptic protagonist. She carries, as Iman Jackson argues, symbolic-material aspects that are attendant with a *black mater*, and disrupts these categories further as the narrative progresses. The protagonist must also reflect on her ceaseless duties as a mother and the dangers she is soon to encounter with regard to confronting the man who will use her traditional and cultural power to destroy her and her mothers. Walking along with the duppy buys Ti-Jeanne time to ruminate on her fear and to consider how she may defeat Rudy. But she is still unable to focus on the impending confrontation because she must, again, care for the infant that is strapped to her body. She realizes the danger in which she is placing the baby, and feels sorrow and attachment as she realized he is the only family left to her, now:

> As they walked, Ti-Jeanne opened her jacket and put Baby to nurse. Her breasts were achingly full. As Baby began to suckle, the familiar draining weariness tugged at Ti-Jeanne, as always when it had been a long time between feedings. Baby's little fist opened and closed against her skin. He looked deeply into her eyes as though he were trying to communicate something. He seemed reluctant to take her breast. He'd suck a little, then spit out the nipple and whimper, staring up at her. She was probably taking him to his death. "Child, I sorry," she whispered at him.... "She gone, doux-doux," she said to him. She'd never used that endearment with him before. But now he was the only one of her family left, unless she counted the disembodied woman who was bound by Rudy's obeah to kill her. "Mami gone." She wanted to cry, but no more tears would come, only a sort of dry, gasping noise. Baby suckled halfheartedly and eventually fell asleep. (174)

This incredible scene illustrates the many directions in which this character is pulled: she must be a mother to her child; must bear her grief at the death of Mami Gros-Jeanne and her own mother, with whom she was reunited only briefly before her body was murdered; and she must bear the guilt and regret of bringing her child on this possibly—or rather, likely—fatal mission. It is precisely these circumstances that highlight Ti-Jeanne as an exceptional protagonist among heroic characters in the genre of post-apocalyptic novels. Alcena Madeline Davis Rogan states that "black women assume the burden of institutionalized sex/race discrimination, as well as sex discrimination within their own families and communities," and as a result "the black woman's relationship to the central formative trope of the culture in which she lives was, and continues to be, necessarily different from the white woman's" (75). The management of particular numerous and critical concerns simultaneously points to the reality of black women in underprivileged contexts in the milieu in which the novel was written: these women must simultaneously manage the care of children in unsafe environments where they are subject to racism and oppression within a colonial history and a system that maintains this oppression. In order to keep their children safe and nourished, these women must take control of their circumstances and eschew cultural maternal expectations and limitations.

Black mothers must operate within a system that is both racist and patriarchal, but the realm of the imaginary allows for hope for a new future, as scholars such as Akhona Nkenkana describe, envisioning the possibility of creating new African futures that re-imagine women's roles, which "should not be reduced to efforts of incorporation of women within the patriarchal, colonial and imperial modern system/s women seek to reject" (41). This novel imagines precisely this future: Ti-Jeanne, a young black mother, takes the reins of patriarchal oppression, embodied and deployed by Rudy, and compels a change—not so that she may rule over the gang, the inner city Burn, and the spirit world herself, but instead so that she can remake her world into one where other mothers may thrive and where those with her abilities may live in mutual accord alongside the beings in the spirit realm. She facilitates the birth of this new world not by means of white cultural values and knowledge, but by means of her Caribbean cultural root beliefs through her relationship with the precolonial pantheon and religion, and with the help of her mother before her—through Gros-Jeanne's reemergence and Mi-Jeanne's assistance.

In spite of enslavement, one black mother finds ways to assist her daughter in achieving her objective and reach freedom. As Ti-Jeanne, Baby, and Tony make their way across the city to reach Rudy's headquarters, the duppy, the remains of Ti-Jeanne's mother, gives them opportunities to escape in spite of being, in many ways, chained to Rudy. Ti-Jeanne's freedom would in many ways lead to freedom for all three mothers, and so "Ti-Jeanne was determined to go to Rudy's place and make an end to this madness, one way or the other" (176). Both this fear and the potential for freedom stretches back in time, and forward into future generations, since "the black woman's relationship to her self and her family must be constantly reevaluated, historicized as a relation degraded by the legacy of her slavery-era status as the literal site of the reproduction of white-owned property" (Madeline Davis Rogan, 75). Ti-Jeanne must quell her fear, though, before she can defeat Rudy, but she is constantly faced not only with the possibility of dying at Rudy's hands, but becoming enslaved by him as her mother is enslaved—a fate worse than death. The intergenerational enslavement of these women by the mob boss echoes the history of slavery that leads to the diaspora culture and magical tradition that the mothers have inherited, and Ti-Jeanne must use this knowledge to push aside her fear and fight for freedom. But the punishments that Rudy inflicts on others who cross him reflect the punishment that slaves suffered historically. Ti-Jeanne is reminded of these punishments whenever she encounters Rudy, such as when she and Tony spot Rudy looking for them as they walk on the city streets:

> Some sense of reality intruded on the false bravado that grief and anger had lent her. What had she been thinking? This was the man who skinned someone alive on a whim! "Not here. We can't meet he here, like this. I not ready." (178)

The horror of Rudy's violence has left unmistakable trauma on those who witness his torture, and the fact that one of his victims is complicit in this violence, Mi-Jeanne the duppy, exacerbates the trauma experienced by observers. Ti-Jeanne and Tony barely escape Rudy and the duppy, but they manage to reach an underground children's enclave where they meet friends who help them and can find a babysitter for Baby. Ti-Jeanne then carries on with her final quest, where she entreats the help of the gods above and spirits below to assist her. Nevertheless, she must constantly contend with her fear, often finding herself "shuddering, nearly out of her mind with pain and fright" (203).

Beyond her maternal drive and motivation to free her mother, which allows her to overcome her fear, Ti-Jeanne draws on her diaspora heritage to empower her. Ti-Jeanne prays to the deity Papa Legbara to send her to the "shores of Guinea Land," so that she will not be visible to human eyes, and asks the same for Rudy. According to Elena Bustamante,

> Hopkinson connects this episode with Afro-Caribbean tradition, as Legbara's strategy consists in hiding the young woman "halfway in Guinea Land" . . . Guinea Land is the mythical land of the ancestors for many Africans transplanted to the Americas, and, as a matter of fact, many African slaves committed suicide during plantation times in order to return to this mythical native land. (22)

Ti-Jeanne asks the spirit Legbara to send her and Rudy to these shores so that they can confront each other without the interference of Rudy's henchmen. And once she does walk into Rudy's building invisible, exiting the elevator with gun in hand, Rudy is surprised but for him, her arrival is not entirely unexpected. Before her entrance, Rudy had said, in disgust, "This is war between me and that Ti-Jeanne woman now" (199) and that this "ruined city was his kingdom. He wasn't going to let Gros-Jeanne's brood take it away from him" (200). His relegation of Ti-Jeanne to "that woman" and even as "that bitch" within the maternal "brood" places him in distinct patriarchal opposition to the three generations of mothers (see "Magical Women and the Threat to Patriarchal Order," below). In order to save mothers, past and future, Ti-Jeanne must defeat the patriarchal order embodied in Rudy.

However, Ti-Jeanne must kill her mother in order to free her and defeat Rudy, a matricide that seems to echo the common mythological motif of patricide. There are numerous examples of this motif, such as the Babylonian Ea's murder of his father Apsu, the Hindu Arjun was killed by his son Babruvahana, and Cronus being killed by his son Zeus in ancient Greek mythology. Yet, these patricides were often motivated by self-interest—the gaining of power, wealth, female possession, or revenge—but that is not the case here. Ti-Jeanne's need to commit matricide is a means of destroying the idea of the old symbolic order, as Judith Butler argues, in which "paternal law structures all linguistic signification, termed 'the symbolic,' and so becomes a universal organizing principle of culture itself" (Butler, "Body Politics," 104). Mi-Jeanne willingly submitted to the "paternal law" by rejecting Gros-Jeanne's empowering, though borderline abusive, obeah education, instead seeking out and submitting to her misogynist, exploitative, and cruelly manipulative father, Rudy. As a result of her submission, he stole her voice and her spirit, literally and figuratively, and compelled her to serve and assist him in his rise to power. This relationship reflects a system of patriarchal power that Rudy attempted to assert over Gros-Jeanne, and one that reverberates throughout the area within Toronto that he dominates—even reaching the Premier herself. Ti-Jeanne's task is to destroy this symbolic system by committing matricide and bringing about a new order, one that, according to Amber Jacobs, overturns

> the paternal symbolic function [and] instead resurrects the mother from the so-called imaginary, presymbolic primitive realm and places her within the social arena of language, representation, and history. Such a move immediately upsets and destabilizes the structure of the oedipal phallic paradigm through which patriarchal power relations are secured. . . . [T]he symbolic function is dislodged from its automatic reference to the father . . . functioning to break up the mother-infant imaginary dyad and thus creating a position from which to think and speak. (XI)

In other words, matricide—too little studied, Jacobs argues—is a literary moment that disrupts the patriarchal relegation of the maternal to history's and culture's proverbial dustbin, and instead places her in central production of culture and demonstrating that she has the ability to overturn the "old order" and instantiate one that she chooses. Ti-Jeanne can only kill her mother by destroying the calabash, the "duppy bowl" that is a metaphorical chalice/vulva that holds Mi-Jeanne's spirit imprisoned within it, refusing to allow the duppy spirit to be reborn into the spiritual realm. Once Mi-Jeanne is freed from what ties her to the vestiges of life, Ti-Jeanne will have made a significant step in instantiating a new order.

Ti-Jeanne must fight with her mother's spirit, and is injured and nearly killed in the conflict, until she remembers that her mother is now a form of soucouyant, which can be tricked. Ti-Jeanne does so, by spraying droplets of blood on the floor so that the duppy must count them. Enraged, Rudy lunges at Ti-Jeanne for deceiving the duppy and him, but the young mother "intuitively . . . fired past him at her mother's prison. *Instinct. Don't think.* The calabash exploded into shards. Noxious things flew from it: reeking clumps of dirt; a twist of hair; white knuckle bones . . . . The duppy swelled, flared to incandescent, its freed hands outstretched in thanks to Ti-Jeanne. It dove at Rudy. . . . But then the duppy shrank to the size of an ember and winked out. Gone. Her mother was finally fully dead, and Ti-Jeanne was alone with Rudy" (204). As the prison exploded, objects that represent the toxicity of Rudy's relationship with his daughter were jettisoned, and the woman's spirit could be finally free from patriarchal domination.

After committing matricide and destroying an aspect of female submission to patriarchal control, Ti-Jeanne must destroy patriarchal oppression itself. After the destruction of the calabash, Rudy immediately begins to age. His unnatural youth, fed from Mi-Jeanne's spirit, disappears, revealing his mortality through

> a network of wrinkles was stitching itself over his face. Swollen veins wormed their way over the backs of his hands, while the knuckles bunched like the knobs of ancient roots; he put his arthritic hands to his mouth, spat his teeth into them. His lips sank in on themselves . . . his hair blanched to grey. (205)

This scene underscores the decline of patriarchal power; the Lacanian symbolic order is an old one and is diminishing before the new paradigm, one that is embodied by a young, black mother. Rudy attempts to stop this transition by declaring that Ti-Jeanne's spirit will now serve as his new duppy. He is able to capture and restrain Ti-Jeanne, and performs a ritual that nearly succeeds. He does separate Ti-Jeanne's spirit from her body temporarily, and as she floats about in the spirit world, she nearly decides to accede to Rudy's plan, blaming her lack of freedom not on the patriarchal order, but on her motherhood:

> What if Tony hadn't been able to slide into Ti-Jeanne's heart. . . . She probably wouldn't have got pregnant. There would be no Baby constantly demanding her attention and her energy. *She coulda go wherever she want, nobody to stop she.* (215)

As she considers the possibilities of this new-found "freedom" as a spirit, the Jab-Jab appears to her, and reminds her that this experience is illusory, that she would always remain subject to Rudy's whims and abuse, compelled to murder human beings in order to feed on the blood that will maintain Rudy's youth. The horrible images Jab-Jab shares with her awaken Ti-Jeanne from her dreamlike state, and she begins to see the reality of her situation:

> Rudy cared nothing for love or loss. What would she be if she became his creature? Hesitantly she said to the Jab-Jab, "I can't keep giving my will into other people hands no more, ain't? I have to decide what I want to do for myself." No answer. It wasn't going to tell her. . . . She looked up, but the Jab-Jab was gone. She had to figure out how to stop Rudy herself. (220)

As is typical in their conversations, the Jab-Jab only points out Ti-Jeanne's situation, and *she* must decide how to move forward.

She makes her decision based on what she remembers of Gros-Jeanne's guidance. She allows her intuition to guide her as well, and her thoughts are drawn to a critical means to invoke the deities, a form of communication that is shared among numerous religions—an axis mundi that serves as *"the centre pole [that] is the bridge between the worlds"* (221). Heinrich Hermann states, when describing objects that initiate moments of connection with the transcendental, that "elements such as . . . *axis mundi,* speak directly, across distances of time and space, to the human understanding of the temporality and continuity of life, and our essential link to the natural world" (39). A significant axis mundi comes to her mind, and

> Ti-Jeanne thought of the centre pole of the palais, reaching up into the air and down toward the ground. She thought of the building she was in. The CN Tower. And she understood what it was: 1,815 feet of the tallest centre pole in the world. Her duppy body almost laughed a silent *kya-kya,* a jokey Jab-Jab laugh. *For like the spirit tree that the centre pole symbolized, the CN Tower dug roots deep into the ground where the dead lived and pushed high into the heavens where the oldest ancestors lived.* The tower was their ladder into this world. A Jab-Jab type of joke, oui. She was halfway into Guinea Land herself.

She could call the spirits to help her. She wouldn't have to call very loudly. (221, emphasis mine)

And at this point Ti-Jeanne calls on the gods, asking them to "come down and help your daughter!" (221).

The maternal heroine invokes non-Western, diaspora deities individually, acknowledging each of them as elements of the Caribbean culture that are so critical to her mission. One by one, she calls their names, and at the forefront of the fight are the goddesses. The tower shakes, lightning erupts from the sky, and Ti-Jeanne sees that

> outside in the miles-high air, Shango Lord Thunder drummed his rhythm while Oya of the storm flashed and shattered the air like knives. Ti-Jeanne had an impression of an ecstatic woman's features, silver dreadlocks tossing wildly as she danced around a hugely muscled, graceful man who clasped a tall drum between his knees. . . . The first of the Oldest Ones had arrived. (222–223)

Oya, the storm goddess, precedes the other deities and draws down the elements that will accompany the gods. The lightning, wind and rain begin to form cracks in the tower, and then "water began to leak in, buckets of it. The water traced forms along the wall, and two majestic Black women stepped out from its current: graceful Oshun and beautiful Emanjah, water goddesses both, anger terrible on their unearthly faces" (223). The goddesses cause both of Rudy's henchmen to suddenly succumb to disease and die. The goddesses react differently to the effects of their power:

> Oshun wrinkled her nose in distaste and fanned her face with the intricate cutwork fan she was holding. . . . She delicately picked up the hem of her white-trimmed yellow robe and stepped out of the way. Her sister Emanjah simply quirked an eyebrow in amusement. The tribal scars shifted on her cheeks when she smiled. Then Ti-Jeanne felt the beneficence of Osain, the healer, leaching the poison from her body. (223)

The deities, specific to the tradition from which Ti-Jeanne's mothers emerged, have manifested corporeally, so that Ti-Jeanne is able to see them in their individual aspects. Further, like the Jeanne mothers, the deities "satirize and destabilize patriarchal power, suggesting through their destructive feminine archetypes the obverse of victimhood and abjection" (Bryce, 7).

She also knows instinctively that she must also call the chthonic spirits of her ancestors and those who were unjustly murdered by Rudy, including those whose body parts were taken to earn a profit on the elite market. The most important of these spirits are her mothers, and the only male figure she remembers from her past with benevolence:

> With a flash of instinct, she knew that the call to the heavens should be mirrored by a call to the earth. "All you children; every one Rudy kill to feed he duppy bowl—come and let we stop he from making another one! Dunston! And Mami! And Mi-Jeanne! Is Ti-Jeanne calling you! Come up, come up and help your daughter! . . . Climb the pole, allyou; climb the pole!" (221)

The earthly spirits climb the axis mundi just as the deities descended it, and they seek vengeance on Ti-Jeanne's behalf. As she calls these earthly spirits, she also returns to her own earthly body: "She wanted to wait in her duppy body to see what would happen, but her flesh body was reeling her in again. Its pain was descending upon her. Like tumbling headfirst into mud, she rejoined her flesh body" (222). Suddenly, Ti-Jeanne is "reborn," having approached the edges of Guinea Land, thus in many ways completing the "Hero's Journey" as defined by Joseph Campbell. By dying and being reborn, Ti-Jeanne completes an entire cycle of heroism in the post-apocalypse. She has also crossed a number of borders, between the apocalyptic degradation of The Burn and outside of it; grasping the importance of the bourn between spiritual and physical realms; and in completing her mission to defeat Rudy, she has confronted the "social and political injustice most readily experienced by persons from diasporic, transitory and migratory communities in the borderlands between the global north and south" (Moynaugh, 212).

After Ti-Jeanne's harrowing ordeal, she returns home—Gros-Jeanne's home—where her friend Jenny is looking after Baby. Ti-Jeanne has just fought her mother's duppy, Rudy's henchmen, then Rudy himself. Her spirit was separated from her body, and she expended energy invoking the deities and the spirits of the dead. Yet, instead of going home to immediate rest, as soon as the baby sees Ti-Jeanne, "he was already rooting hungrily at her breast. Ti-Jeanne unbuttoned her jacket, yanked up her shirt, and gave him the nipple" (245). Ti-Jeanne, thus, again complicates assumptions about heroic *nostos*, not receiving a "hero's welcome" in a conventional manner, but instead embracing her infant and breastfeeding him.

SUPERNATURAL CARIBBEAN MATERNAL LEGACY

The protagonist of *Brown Girl in the Ring* is a formidable hero who does not summon her power from a source of unknown internal capacity that she has just discovered, but instead summons a heritage, passed on through generations of mothers, that calls upon non-Western origins. The elements of

African-diasporic "mythologies" are exalted as the means by which the protagonist grows in strength and defeats the patriarchal oppression of her grandfather and her former lover. This belief system, originally emerging from the Yoruba religion that traveled from West Africa to the Caribbean through the slave trade, is one that Ti-Jeanne inherits, though she initially rejects her ancestral legacy. Once she embraces this heritage, though, she calls upon deities that are born from the Yoruba religious diaspora, deities that survived the attempted Christianization of the slave population who held onto

> the power icons represented by African divine forces. In Haitian *vodun*, Brazilian *candomble*, Trinidad's *orisha* or *shango*, and Cuban *regla de ocha* and *palo monte* . . . deities and ancestors were and still are invoked for help and guidance. The conviction that the body may be hurt but the spirit strengthened by trials and eventually freed by death. (Warner-Lewis, 121)

It is precisely this belief that empowers Ti-Jeanne through her trials as a mother and fighter against oppression: she invokes the deities in the depths of her fear or at the cusp of her surrender, even as her spirit separates from her physical body, which for the Christian religion would mean the end of life, but for Ti-Jeanne her spirit's separation is a playful jaunt, when briefly "her duppy body claimed air as its home" until she is compelled to return (217).

By centering the protagonist's power in non-Western narrative traditions, Hopkinson draws upon what Walter Mignolo refers to as "de-linking," in which

> places of nonthought (of myth, non-western religions, folklore, underdevelopment involving regions and people) today have been waking up from the long process of westernization. The *anthropos* inhabiting non-European places discovered that s/he had been invented, as *anthropos*, by a locus of enunciations self-defined as *humanitas*. (3)

In other words, Hopkinson's novel brings about a realization of the contrivance of heroes as Western non-mothers, thereby rejecting "the *former anthropos* who are no longer claiming *recognition by* or *inclusion in*, the *humanitas*, but engaging in epistemic disobedience and de-linking from the magic of the Western idea of modernity, ideals of humanity" (Mignolo, 3). Hopkinson's narrative de-linking is an illustration of what Mignolo argues inverts the Western suppositions of who may "save the world," and by what means. In the post-collapse landscape of a future Toronto, Western assumptions based in science and capitalist interests form the bedrock of magical thinking, and it is by means of the Caribbean orisha spirit world that there exists the hope that the world may be saved.

As Ti-Jeanne makes her way through her neighborhood, the "Burn," she meets a number of others who know her but their conversation focus is often not on Ti-Jeanne, but instead on Gros-Jeanne, Ti-Jeanne's grandmother, who practices Caribbean *obeah* magic and pharmaceutical herbalism. Early in the novel, during one of these neighborhood walks, she is given herbal plants to deliver to her grandmother in exchange for Gros-Jeanne's medicinal products. Traditionally, according to the narrator, the ingredients would remain secret, not handed out by those who consume them: "Among Caribbean people, bush medicine used to be something private, but living in the Burn changed all the rules" (14).

As a Caribbean woman, and particularly a mother, in her family's lineage, Ti-Jeanne possesses supernatural insight. She is periodically possessed by images that display to her the manner in which others will die. For example, when she encounters one of Rudy's henchmen on the street,

> abruptly, the visions were there again. Ti-Jeanne froze, not trusting her eyes any longer to pick reality from fantasy. . . . Crack Monkey . . . falling to the ground and gasping his last . . . Crapaud . . . in a run-down privatized hospital, finding the strength to scratch fitfully once more at his bedsores before his final, rattly exhalation . . . Jay, killed by love . . . [But] Ti-Jeanne couldn't see her own death, or Baby's . . . not anyone close to her. (16–17)

This disturbing ability will cause her significant anxiety, but also allows her to "see" how to emerge from the life-or-death situations she finds herself in throughout the novel. The visions remain frightful to her until she ultimately embraces her heritage, or in Gros-Jeanne's words, "serves the spirits," and she then understands that the visions are a gift from her patron deity, Legbara.

The visions do not only allow her to see the deaths of individuals she encounters. She also finds herself suddenly overcome by her visions and subsequently immersed by a liminal space between her world and the spirit world, the "shores of Guinea land." While standing in a restaurant, for example, she suddenly

> appeared to be in a green tropical meadow. . . . A figure came over the rise. . . . *Man-like, man-tall, on long, wobbly legs look as if they hitch on backward* . . . [Baby] chortled and stretched baby-fat hands out in the direction of the Jab-Jab. . . . Lately the visions had been growing stronger, more vivid . . . Ti-Jeanne felt the gears slipping between the two worlds. (18–19)

Only Ti-Jeanne and Baby see the spirit figures, pointing to their inherent abilities as descendants of Caribbean obeah practitioners. These scenes of sudden manifestation in realms outside of her reality allude to a connection that is inescapable, whether she embraces the maternal legacy or not, and that she must also negotiate the liminal of the diaspora and the West.

The spirit apparitions that Ti-Jeanne encounters, although an inherent part of the Caribbean culture that she is born into, also point to the colonial "knowledges" that have alienated Ti-Jeanne from them, and relegated the orishas to an unacceptable non-Western non-Christian practice. Walter Mignolo points out the ways in which Christianity is very much integrated into the colonial project, and states that

> Knowledge-making entrenched with imperial/colonial purposes, from the European Renaissance to the US neoliberalism . . . was grounded—as mentioned before—in specific languages, institutions and geo-historical locations. The languages of Western imperial/knowledge-making (and the self-definition of the West—the West of Jerusalem—by social actors that saw themselves as Western Christians) were practiced (speaking and writing) by social actors (human beings) dwelling in a specific geo-historical space, with specific memories that said actors constructed and reconstructed in the process of creating their own Christian, Western and European identity. (18)

This Christian, Western, European identity was imposed on colonized peoples for their own "benefit" to remake them closer to the Western ideal, and thus closer to human, necessitating the vilification and destruction of the imperial subject's native beliefs. In the words of Frantz Fanon, the colonized person's "metaphysics, or, less pretentiously, his customs and the sources on which they were based, were wiped out because they were in conflict with a civilization that he did not know and that imposed itself on him" (83). We see this internalized colonization and slow return to colonized-Caribbean roots taking place in the experience of Ti-Jeanne, particularly in her interactions with the Jab-jab and with her mother.

The figure, the "Jab-jab," gets its name from the French "Diable-diable," placing the spirit figure in the colonial context of a "devil." However, as is clear later in the novel, as Ti-Jeanne grows to accept her magical abilities, the spirit creature becomes a benevolent one, undermining the pejorative name given to it by colonial belief/value system. In her first encounter with the Jab-Jab, Ti-Jeanne looks upon the apparition with horror, even covering Baby's eyes. However, as described above, Baby feels no horror at all, and reaches out to the spirit (19). The distinction between the reactions of mother and child when encountering the Jab-Jab are critical to note, and demonstrate that the Jab-Jab is not inherent wicked or frightening, but is only seen this way by someone who has been implicitly or explicitly taught to fear such creatures. By the novel's conclusion, Ti-Jeanne recognizes the deity as her "Eshu," or as "Legbara."

Caribbean Yoruba folklore is an integral element of the narrative, forming a real and concrete aspect of the novel that the protagonist must navigate. One evening, after breastfeeding and laying her child down to sleep for the night, Ti-Jeanne hears steps behind her:

> *A fireball whirl in through the window glass like if the glass ain't even there . . . and turn into a old, old woman. . . . She flesh red and wet and oozing all over, . . . laughing kya-kya like Mami does do when something sweet she, but I ain't want to know what could sweet a Soucouyant so.* (44)

A soucouyant is a Caribbean folklore character that appears to humans as a fireball after peeling away its crone-like skin, and can only be deterred by presenting it with rice or sugar, the grains of which the spirit creature is compelled to count. The soucouyant sucks the blood of its victims, and "the soucouyant myth might originally have been used during scientifically underdeveloped times to explain mysterious deaths, especially those of babies" (Anatol, "Soucouyants," 34). When the soucouyant appears before Ti-Jeanne, the young mother recognizes her immediately and understands what this means for her child. Despite her fear, she stands between the hag-spirit and the sleeping baby, when "another figure ran in through the doorway on the jokey backward legs. *Oh God, not the Jab-Jab!*" (45). However, despite its diabolical name, the Jab-Jab confronts not Ti-Jeanne, but the Soucouyant:

> Brandishing his stick to block her way, the Jab-Jab threw something to the ground from the other hand—rice grains? . . . The Soucouyant stiffened up when she saw the rice, then dropped to her knees. . . . Now the Jab-Jab was dancing around the Soucouyant, hitting her with the stick. (45)

This scene reveals that the misunderstood Jab-Jab is not a *Diable-Diable* at all, but instead is a spirit protector who arrives in time to save the mother's child. The Jab-Jab continues to injure the Soucouyant with his stick, and then tells Ti-Jeanne to throw open the curtains and allow the morning light to shine on the monster. She immediately dissolves in smoke and ash.

Clearly the Caribbean spirit, named after the Christian paradigm of evil, proves itself to, in fact, perform the protective duties of a guardian angel. This undermining of Western Christian assumptions is a significant statement by the author—it is engagement and reconnection with these deities that imbues one with power and disregarding or shunning them can be detrimental. In one of the most critical scenes in the novel, Ti-Jeanne has decided that she must confront the wicked and powerful Rudy in order to bring about a safer world for those she cares about and stop his exploitation of obeah and the spirit world. She walks up to the lofty tower that has come to be known as

"Rudy's office," and is momentarily dizzied by its soaring height, adding to the monumentality of her task. She is immobilized from fear, paralyzed because "I frighten too bad" (191). But she then hears a voice that breaks into her trance, and she sees the

> Jab-Jab standing there. . . . It just bust a grin and say, 'You coming?' It run up to one of the deep, curving walls of the tower and it start to climb up the side . . . "I have to, yes. I can't make this go on no longer." . . . All this time it been haunting me, and now is the first time I find voice enough to speak to it. (191)

In order to rescue the future for her child, Ti-Jeanne must defeat Rudy, but it is the Jab-Jab who dissipates her fear and reminds her of her task. And the task is hers, as the Jab-Jab reminds her—nearly all who have helped and encouraged her so far have died or been injured, including her maternal predecessors Gros-Jeanne and Mi-Jeanne. The Jab-Jab reminds her of this when he says, "You have to stop he, you know. . . . Is only you leave. Is up to little Ti-Jeanne. Gros-Jeanne dead and Mi-Jeanne get trapped. Is up to little Ti-Jeanne" (192). The Jab-Jab helps her to calmly think through what she needs to do, waiting patiently as she reasons that she cannot stop Rudy by overpowering him, but must trick him instead. Once she has reached this conclusion and has formed a plan, the Jab-Jab cements her realization that she has the power to defeat Rudy on her own by abandoning her: "The Jab-Jab had disappeared when she wished she could become invisible again. Said it didn't need to tell her any more. Maybe she could do it, then" (193). Thus, the entity that was historically maligned by white Western culture is precisely who leads Ti-Jeanne to the realization that she can defeat evil—the embodiment of patriarchy and oppression—on her own.

There are other apparitions who come to Ti-Jeanne's aid, each demonstrating not only the power of the women who inherently possess the ability to invoke assistance from deities, but also each woman's connection with a culture that is distant geographically and chronologically. Ti-Jeanne resides in Toronto, Canada, a significant distance from her cultural home. She is also two generations removed from a practitioner of obeah who was trained within the culture that recognizes this magical practice. Nevertheless, such spirits as the Jab-Jab and her "Eshu," or Legbara, remind her of her power and her abilities to change the fates of her child and her mothers, even after their "death." An Eshu, as Ti-Jeanne refers to the deity Legbara, is a messenger between humans and gods, and is a trickster in some Caribbean folktales. For example, when she asks Legbara to make her and Rudy invisible, in order to trick him, this means of victory by tricking a more powerful being fits precisely into the trickster tradition that Eshu Legbara exemplifies. In one scene, she is even possessed by the spirit in order to save her from Rudy's henchmen: "And then

Ti-Jeanne chuckled in a deep, rumbling voice, the same unearthly sound that she'd made in the chapel. . . . She suddenly seemed much taller than Jay . . . Ti-Jeanne/Prince of Cemetery took a daddy-long-legs step over to him . . . picked him up like a baby and *cradled* him to its bony chest . . . 'Crick Crack Monkey,' came the Prince of Cemetery's voice," and when she/it tells them to be gone, one of the asks Ti-Jeanne "And who the rass are you to be giving Rudy orders, woman?" (117–118). The deity answers, "Woman, man, child? Is all one when them come to me in the end . . . Tell Rudy him know me . . . Tell him this horse is my daughter. Him not to harm she. You go remember my name . . . Legbara. The Eshu da Capa Preta" (118). The deity, a form of psychopomp, states in Portuguese that he inhabits the "crossroads," and is "referring to the Brazilian name for Maît' Carrefour and the Ghede, the same 'Exu da Capa Preta' who is used for creating duppy spirits and taking the dead over to the other side, protects Ti-Jeanne" (Coleman, 11). Ti-Jeanne was first aware of the Eshu Legbara when she observes her Mami Gros-Jeanne invoke the spirit, but the deity has accompanied her from the narrative's beginning, as her deathly visions indicate.

Once Ti-Jeanne accepts her guardian deity, she learns to call upon it. Recalling when she observed her Mami Gros-Jeanne invoke the spirit of the Eshu Legbara, Ti-Jeanne attempts to call the spirit Legbara to help her in the novel's most critical moments—as she forms a plan to reach and confront Rudy. Instead of attempting to compel the spirit to serve her, as Rudy has done, she gathers the elements of an offering to cajole the spirit into assisting her. Her Mami Gros-Jeanne offered the spirit fine rum and a cigar, but Ti-Jeanne has neither of those things, instead only able to offer peppermints and a stale cigarette. But her intentions are assured, and she additionally places herself in the line of mothers who have attempted to defeat Rudy and stop his evil exploitation, which is a mission that the deity supports:

> "Papa Legbara," she whispered, feeling foolish, "I going to try and end the work that Mami and Mi-Jeanne couldn't finish. I going to try and stop Rudy." She knew that by calling the spirit "Papa," she was acknowledging a bond between them. Strangely, that felt safe and right, not the imposition on her that she had thought it would be. That gave her the courage to say a little more: "Help me, please, Papa, and I go make a proper meal for you. Send me to the shores of Guinea Land again, so I could get into Rudy office without anyone seeing me."
> . . . She waited long minutes to see if Legbara would accept her gift. (195)

By aligning her plans with the intergenerational task of these three mothers—crone, mother, maiden—she will close the circle that will end the terrible oppression of the patriarchal mob boss, Rudy, and free all of the spirits trapped by him.

The deities that Ti-Jeanne calls to aid her are not only male but include important female figures. The goddess that stands out among the others is the mother goddess Emanjah, who also appears as Yemojah and Yemanja, among other names, in other cultures in the African diaspora. Emanjah is the first goddess to be invoked by Ti-Jeanne after she calls forth a number of gods. She also calls Oya, a Yoruba goddess of death and storms; Oshun, a goddess of beauty and water; but Emanjah, a goddess of motherhood, pregnancy, and water, is first among them, and like Ti-Jeanne's patron deity Jab-Jab/Legbara, she sees the conflict between the deities and Rudy with humor: "Emanjah simply quirked an eyebrow in amusement. The tribal scars shifted on her cheeks when she smiled" (223). The god Jab-Jab/Legbara brings forth the spirits of the children, whose murders were caused by Rudy, and he causes their deaths, and the deaths of everyone Rudy killed, to fall upon him, causing his body to fall apart. Ti-Jeanne is sickened by the sight, and the god Osain reminds her that she carries Rudy's blood in her. Emanjah steps in, and her

> deep, warm voice interrupted. "Nah give the child any more to fret about, Osain. Me know say she not going forget is who blood she come from." It was Emanjah. Her blue-and-white robes clung to her ample body like water droplets on skin. She was very beautiful. "Sister," she said to Oshun, "help me wash away this garbage, please." (226)

Her "ample" body alludes to her iconic status as a goddess of the maternal, and the fact that she releases water into the room is a sort of breaking of the amniotic fluid, washing away the remnants of patriarchal oppression and making way for Ti-Jeanne's rebirth into a liberated new world that she—with the help of the divine assembly she called forth—has brought about. As the goddess departs along with the waters she summoned, Ti-Jeanne notices the destroyed human bodies are gone, since "Emanjah had taken them away. Ti-Jeanne felt a longing pull at her. Emanjah's voice had had something of her mother's in it" (227). The longing she feels is a resonance with the mother goddess whose voice echoes that of her mother, her mother's mother, and her own inner maternal voice.

The veritable pantheon of deities that accompany, befriend, and protect Ti-Jeanne (and the mothers before her), illustrate what Shireen Roshanravan describes as an "insertion within African-diasporic spiritual communities to generate feminist ways of knowing based in African cosmologies that endured . . . colonization" (44). Ti-Jeanne does not set out on her quest to generate a feminist perspective, of course, and must incessantly battle her fear of Rudy and her inclination to quit and run as far as she can from him. But by placing her trust in a pantheon that "disobeys" the culture that surrounds her, Ti-Jeanne is able to break free of and defeat the narrative's oppressive patriarch, and goes on to re-form a world in which future mothers—and her former ones—can be empowered.

MAGICAL WOMEN AND THE THREAT TO PATRIARCHAL ORDER

"Witchy women" are undeniably threatening to the Symbolic order, and are often punished in a tortuous manner in the public sphere.[1] Ronald Hutton states this anxiety well, in his 2017 treatise on witch-hunt history, stating that modern-day reactionaries believe that those accused of witchcraft often "were still adherents" and "deserved to be punished and repressed," while

> feminists could reverse these claims by portraying the pagan witch religions as being a joyous, life-affirming, liberating one which . . . elevated the status of women, strongest among the common people and pitted against everything that the established Churches, aristocracies and patriarchies represented; which is why . . . the latter brutally crushed it. (120)

The life-affirming and liberating characteristics of the female magical practitioners in Hopkinson's novel are apparent when viewed in opposition to perpetrators of patriarchal oppression. Gros-Jeanne rejects her abusive spouse instead of fearing him, and Ti-Jeanne stands up to her manipulative former lover after her grandmother's spiritual training engenders her empowerment. The most powerful male character in this novel, the only one who practices this particular form of obeah, wields it unnaturally by imprisoning souls to feed an unnatural youthful strength and vigor, yet his absconded abilities are not questioned by any other character in the novel. The female characters acquire the ability to employ obeah without seeking this power, "witchcraft" comes naturally to them, and these women tend to use it in the traditional Caribbean purpose, for healing and otherworldly prophecy. Ti-Jeanne, at first, rejects this aspect of her nature, but when she finally accepts her Mami Gros-Jeanne's instruction, she—as does the reader, by proxy—learns critical lessons about her culture that has survived colonial attempted destruction:

> To start off, it have eight names you must know . . . Shango, Ogun, Osain, Shakpana, Emanjah, Oshun, Oya, and Eshu . . . The African powers, child. The spirits. The loas. The orishas. The oldest ancestors. You will hear people from Haiti and Cuba and Brazil and so call them different names. You will even hear some names I ain't tell you, but we all mean the same thing. . . . Each of we have a special one who is we father or mother, and no matter what we call it,

whether Shango or Santeria or Voudun or what, we all doing the same thing. Serving the spirits. (126)

Thus begins Ti-Jeanne's education, one that points to her destiny that will save both her oppressed people and the "Old Ones." As Gros-Jeanne instructs:

> "The spirits don't call unless we ready to accept the call, so you must be ready, even if you don't want to accept it. Legbara is your guardian . . . if you is a good daughter." And a good daughter single-handedly hunted down obeah-wielding gang lords, Ti-Jeanne supposed. (127)

Further, the good daughter must carry out her destiny, a rescuer of those who have survived into Toronto's dystopia, with a child in tow.

However, from the first appearances of the women's supernatural abilities, they are addressed with mistrust and fear by nearly all of characters who interact with them. For example, when the father of Ti-Jeanne's child, Tony, first encounters Mami Gros-Jeanne in the narrative, she pierces him with the "evil eye," and Ti-Jeanne notes that Gros-Jeanne's

> tiny, fierce body had seemed to tower over Tony's six-foot frame . . . Tony was terrified of the small-boned seer woman . . . for all his medical training and his Canadian upbringing, he'd learned the fear of Caribbean obeah at his mother's knee. His face went grey . . . and [he] hastened away. (26–27)

The knowledge of the significance of obeah gnosis was passed on to the young man by his mother, and whatever power he may feel entitled to as a male in a patriarchal context, alongside the dismissive white culture in which he was raised and educated, disintegrates before the magic of the "seer woman." His instant retreat when confronted by the woman's glance points to the ways that, as Helen Tiffin states, "the black female body is allegorised as lost through a European textuality so deeply interpellative that black 'prince charmings' cannot conceive of or cope with Afro-Caribbean female bodies—their substance has been relegated to a legendary outline . . . European textuality/ slavery has rendered the black male unable to see black women who have been disembodied by that same history," yet, as we see in Hopkinson's narrative, these men may be reminded of black women's power by "an (oral) tradition of a different kind, attesting to the persistence of an Afro-Caribbean folk history/ herstory which frequently (though not exclusively) was preserved and passed on by women" (911). This confrontation with the cultural maternal herstory reflects the vein in which the entire novel is written—suffused with Caribbean folk elements that reconstruct the black mother's body from the attempted destruction wrought by deleterious patriarchy and colonial history.

Tony, the often hapless and manipulated father of Ti-Jeanne's child, is subject to the abuses of Rudy, who is the criminal mastermind behind the nefarious gang that runs Toronto's inner city. The magical mothers Jeanne stand in opposition to Rudy, who makes no secret of his bitterness toward women in general, and the Jeannes in particular. Throughout the novel, his rage directed at the women is cruel, almost to an exaggerated degree, and he derides their connection to the spirit realm: "Rudy was sure he could give the man the right incentive [to kill the women]. And it would get those blasted women and their nicey-nicey balm-yard spirits out of his way once and for all" (129). Rudy's rage causes him to blame the women for the difficulties he faces, leading him to cry out in an oft-repeated lament: "Ti-Jeanne, Mi-Jeanne, Gros-Jeanne; them fucking women been giving me trouble from since when!" (133). Indeed, the "trouble" began before he acquired his supernatural power, when he makes no secret of the fact that he was once married to Gros-Jeanne, whom he abused: "Me wife and all kick me out of me own house. Blasted cow . . . . Just because me give she little slap two-three time when she make she mouth run away 'pon me" (131). Justifiably rejected by his spouse, Rudy vengefully called on the spirits:

> Me call the Eshu. The One in the Black Cape, just like me wife did show me . . . and me tell him me want him to kill everybody that do me bad . . . . Him say all right, if is death I want to deal in . . . Him tell me must find a dead in the cemetery . . . me must call the dead man duppy, and make him serve me . . . . He tell me if I do alla that, neither him nor the rest of the ancestors go want nothing more to do with me. Well . . . what the ancestors ever do for me before? (132)

Thus, Rudy begins the process of exploiting the "duppy" spirits wrenched from the bodies of the recent dead, who help him unjustly kill others, including his former wife's new lover, and the deaths feed Rudy's elderly body, which begins to grow unnaturally rejuvenated, allowing him to take over the criminal posse that now runs inner Toronto and acquire enough power that he even holds sway over Premier Catherine Uttley.

It is clear that Rudy is the dystopian embodiment of oppression of women and sexism with regard to their capabilities and power. Because he has exploited the knowledge of obeah from Gros-Jeanne, his ex-lover, he believes that he can dominate the women who traditionally possess this magical ability. His exploitative power stands alongside the exploitation by the Western culture and its colonial past. Rudy's behavior and seizing of power from the female characters and from the spirit realm echoes such figures as the ancient Greek deity, Zeus, whose treatment of women seems to have, in part, instantiated or echoed the patriarchal roots of Western culture, despite the presence of powerful goddesses. As Amber Jacobs describes in her book *On Matricide: Myth, Psychoanalysis, and the Law of the Mother*,

> Zeus achieves his power through . . . incorporation, and appropriation of the woman/mother. He cannibalizes . . . in order to rob her of knowledge and wisdom, together with her reproductive capacity. From then on, she is silent and invisible, an internal source of power that Zeus will claim as his own. Her existence is obliterated so that not even her own daughter will ever know of the maternal body in which she was originally conceived. Zeus, in his violent operation, succeeds in taking total possession of the (m)other, whose power he both envies and desires. (63)

This description of the patriarch of the gods in Western mythology could easily describe the approach of Rudy in *Brown Girl in the Ring*: he envies Gros-Jeanne's power and takes that power by unnatural means, he then sees the potential in "incorporating" his daughter's spirit which has an inherent connection to the spirit world, and in doing so, takes away her existence to such a degree that even Ti-Jeanne is ignorant of the fact that the mindless woman wandering the streets is her own mother. Rudy is the patriarchal and colonial attempt to excise the maternal power that is in connection with the spirits and the old ways in order to employ this ability for himself, to reinstate the paternal power that he feels has been stolen, thus robbing and silencing the voices that are the source of his "trouble."

But the obeah and the spirits cannot perpetually condone someone who seeks to use this power for the exploitation of others, whether those others are human, spirit, or deity. They recognize the latent power of Ti-Jeanne, a descendant of powerful mothers, and the deities confront her with visions and visitations until, over time, she grows to see them as benevolent. But the one who must point her in the right direction and instruct her on how best to embrace her cultural roots is Mami Gros-Jeanne. The character who most embodies maternal magical practice and wisdom is doubtlessly Gros-Jeanne, the elder of the three Jeanne mothers. She has a number of "titles" to describe her role, as the Jab-Jab relates to Ti-Jeanne in one of their final conversations:

> "You ever ask your grandmother what she was?" the Jab-Jab said. "She was a seer woman," Ti-Jeanne replied . . . "Yes, it have plenty names for what Gros-Jeanne was. Myalist, bush doctor, iyalorisha, curandera, four-eye, even obeah woman for them who don't understand . . . Gros-Jeanne woulda tell you that all she doing is serving the spirits." (219)

This relationship with the spirit world is what sets Gros-Jeanne apart from the other characters who have access to the deities. Unlike her daughter and, for most of the narrative, her granddaughter, Gros-Jeanne does not reject the apparitions that appear to her, and instead lives a life that embraces her spiritual connections and the "old ways," lending her their approbation and also their power. Despite this power, however, she is murdered by Ti-Jeanne's former lover Tony, but her death allows her the opportunity to perform the necessary role of de-linking from colonial oppression, and to continue to assist the disadvantaged and the oppressed and to cease the oppression and exploitation of her people in the Burn community. She does this through the body of a corrupt white authority, the Premier of Ontario, Catherine Uttley.

Premier Uttley makes clear her primary concern resides in the benefit of corporate interests that now reside outside of the dilapidated Toronto city center. In the novel's Prologue, a representative for Premier Uttley approaches Rudy, asking him to find a new human heart for Uttley, since her heart is failing and she does not want to make use of the Porcine Organ Harvest Program that had been designed for this purpose. Rudy chooses Tony—due to his medical training—to seek out a heart, and that heart will come from the body of Gros-Jeanne, whose physiological profile is similar to Uttley's—and she is the cause of so much of Rudy's anxiety. Tony is resistant at first, but like the majority of the inner Toronto Burn population, he is addicted to the drug called Buff, and so he is easily manipulated by the criminal kingpin Rudy to murder Gros-Jeanne and preserve her heart until it can reach the Premier. What Rudy is unaware of, however, is that Gros-Jeanne's heart preserves her spirit within it, and it is by means of this heart that the apocalyptic collapse of the inner city is turned around. An embodiment of Caribbean culture, Gros-Jeanne takes possession of the paradigm of the white colonial, Premier Uttley, and alongside Ti-Jeanne's heroism Gros-Jeanne overturns the collapse and suffering of the Burn and introduces a new civilization that places empathy and humanity at the forefront. This overturning of the exploitative authority is a metaphoric illustration of de-linking from the imperial mindset that can bring about a foregrounding of the interests and well-being of the oppressed.

As the reader and, ultimately, Ti-Jeanne, realize by the novel's conclusion, the revivification of the Burn within Toronto's urban center *requires* the sacrifice of the powerful maternal life, Gros-Jeanne—a form of martyrdom on behalf of the poor and downtrodden. The transplant of Gros-Jeanne's heart catalyzes a new form of "colonization," as the narrative description makes apparent:

> When Wright transplanted the heart, *white* blood cells from Uttley's bone marrow should migrate smoothly into the *foreign organ*, and vice versa, a chimerism that would *trick her* immune system into *accepting the foreign organ* so that body and heart *could coexist peacefully.* (167–168, emphasis added)

This colonization, taking place microcosmically, illustrates the deception that is involved in the process of white bodies colonizing the "foreign" terrain in order to gain the acceptance of the indigenous entities and "live peacefully"—peace emerging from a relationship based on deceit.

While this occupation is taking place within the newly implanted organ, the heart itself is entering a foreign body, and has a very different effect. When Uttley awakens from her organ transplant surgery, her policy advisor notices a difference in her behavior. She tells him, "listen, Constantine, I'm going to change my tactics a little. . . . It's just occurred to me; this volunteer organ donation thing will never work. Human beings will never be eager to deed away bits of themselves, even after they're dead," . . . Constantine frowned at her. "Excuse my bluntness, Premier, but when did you develop a social conscience?" (238). Her newly implanted empathy extends beyond the exploitation of human organs, as she subsequently reveals. Uttley decides that she will place the needs of the residents of the Burn before corporate interests—a strategy that had not been tried before and that is shocking to the Premier's pro-corporate backers:

> "There's another thing, too. We're going to rejuvenate Toronto."
> "Premier, you know that project has always been death to politicians. No one's been able to do it yet."
> "Yeah, 'cause they've tried it by providing incentives for big business to move back in and take over. We're going to offer interest-free loans to small enterprises that are already there, give them perks if they fix up the real estate they're squatting on."
> "What small enterprises? The place is a rat hole, complete with rats."
> "Oh, I don't know. Something tells me we'll discover that there are quite a few resourceful people left in Muddy York." (240)

The values based on the dehumanization of the Burn residents, revealed in the advisor's appalled reaction to Premier Uttley's idea, illustrates the distinction of her present perspective from her previous mindset before receiving Gros-Jeanne's heart. As the novel's Prologue makes clear, corporate interests—and thus government support—in the post-apocalyptic inner city have fled to the suburbs, where profit is still possible:

> When Toronto's economic base collapsed, investors, commerce, and government withdrew into the suburb cities, leaving the rotten core to decay. Those who stayed were the ones who couldn't or wouldn't leave. The street people. The poor people . . . it sparked large-scale chaos in the city core . . . Rudy ruled with his posse now. (4)

After receiving the new heart and Gros-Jeanne's spirit, Uttley seeks to rejuvenate the heart of Toronto just as her own body has been rejuvenated.

The distinction between the Premier's current and former values also foregrounds the motivations behind colonization with regard to the African diaspora in the Caribbean, which is informed by a culture taken from its homeland through enslaved bodies by a profit-seeking empire. The maternal history that distinguishes the Premier from that of the spirit now coexisting in her body is critical to acknowledge, since the

> legacy of the past that the U.S. black woman must contend with is her status within the slavery system both as an object of property and as the hypersexualized site of the reproduction of the slavery system. These roles continue to haunt black women, although they manifest themselves in different ways. (Madeline Davis Rogan, 76)

This history is implicit in the value of one woman's life over another's: Gros-Jeanne's body was slaughtered for a profit-seeking purpose, but her "dark" history was one she carried with her as a Caribbean immigrant in Toronto. Whereas Gros-Jeanne formerly inhabited the Western body of Toronto, she now occupies the white body of Premier Uttley. The sacrifice of her previous body and the subsequent possession of the white body will bring about a transformation that compels the city residents to acknowledge the value of life versus capitalist corporatist interests—a new de-colonial path. As Mignolo states,

> A common topic of conversation today . . . is "how to save capitalism." A de-colonial question would be: "Why would you want to save capitalism and not save human beings? Why save an abstract entity and not the human lives that capitalism is constantly destroying?" In the same vein, geo- and body-politics of knowledge, de-colonial thinking and the de-colonial option place human lives and life in general first. (20)

Certainly, by occupying the body of Premier Uttley, Gros-Jeanne is able to make an enormous beneficial difference for her community and her daughter by compelling the white body to choose the de-colonial option by placing the lives of the residents—rather that corporate non-life—first.

Unlike Ti-Jeanne, Mi-Jeanne definitively turned her back on her maternal obeah legacy, and as a result, she lost touch with the feminine power that would allow her to resist the embodiment of oppressive patriarchy—her own father, Rudy. Yet, she is rescued by her daughter when her duppy is freed from Rudy's prison, and near the novel's conclusion, Ti-Jeanne discovers that her mother's body did not die—the bullet wound was not fatal to her body. After Ti-Jeanne's harrowing ordeal, she returns home—Gros-Jeanne's house—where her friend Jenny is looking after Baby, and Ti-Jeanne finds that Jenny is not only watching over the infant, but also Mi-Jeanne, whose spirit was happily able to return to her human body. This discovery is overwhelming: "A mother found, lost, then found again. This final shock was too much. Ti-Jeanne went into her grandmother's room. Jenny settled her on her side in the bed, so she could feed Baby as she slept" (250). This surprising and happy ending allows for the "resurrection" of all maternal generations, who have repossessed bodies in order to continue—and even accelerate—their transformative maternal work with regard to their post-apocalyptic context.

Although Gros-Jeanne's daughter and granddaughter inherited her abilities in spite of their misgivings, Gros-Jeanne did establish and guide willing followers in her beliefs and practices who follow in her footsteps as servants of the spirits. Jenny was one of those followers and students, and made it clear that she would be able to continue Ti-Jeanne's education in the old ways. She begins by teaching Ti-Jeanne the ways to treat the recently dead:

> It was Jenny who had insisted on the nine-night, a wake for the recently dead that would calm the dead spirit and point out its way to Guinea Land, sent off with the love of the living it must leave behind. "This is how your granny would have wanted it," Jenny told them. "A shasto, a party, to send her soul off with joy. This is her way." Thank God for Mami's flock, eager to teach Ti-Jeanne their rituals. They would hold the ceremony in the palais and, afterward, a feast for anyone who cared to come. (242)

This gratitude demonstrates that Ti-Jeanne will, indeed, continue the spiritual education begun by Gros-Jeanne.

In addition, many of Gros-Jeanne's former patients bring gifts in remembrance and gratitude for Gros-Jeanne, gifts that draw a connection with the Caribbean homeland. These include old man Butler's Caribbean sorrel bush beverage, made from a fruit that cannot grow in Canada's climate. Other gifts are directed to Ti-Jeanne from the spirit world. After Ti-Jeanne's quest, she almost immediately begins to treat the ill and injured from the Burn, and so "Ti-Jeanne and her mother dispensed medicine and tried to keep an eye . . . on Baby. Ti-Jeanne heard herself mutter a 'Thank you' to her dead grandmother for insisting that she learn how to treat the sick" (244). She realizes, though, that the many who come to her home seeking help are actually sent from her patron deity, as when one patient

> sneezed, "Eshu!" Briefly Ti-Jeanne could see his bones through his flesh. Another vision, a joke from her spirit father. She laughed. "Legbara, is you

sending me all these sick people to treat, ain't?" No answer. "Well, Papa, look my answer here. I go do this for a little while, but I ain't Mami. I ain't know what I want to do with myself yet, but I can't be she." (244)

Ti-Jeanne emphasizes the fact that she will not have her destiny written for her, no matter what pressures she receives from her community and the spirit world, but through the education she receives from the spirits and from those serving the spirits, she will continue to change the post-apocalyptic landscape into one that benefits all of her community.

CONCLUSION

In her novel's acknowledgments, Hopkinson thanks "Derek Walcott for writing his play *Ti-Jean and His Brothers* [(1958)], one of the first examples of Caribbean magical realism I have ever read" (249). Hopkinson's novel is a response to Derek Walcott's play, which tells the story of three archetypal heroic brothers in a folktale setting who attempt to defeat the devil. Ti-Jean ultimately wins, due to his embrace of traditional Caribbean culture, his acceptance of help from animals and other humans, and his regard for his mother. Hopkinson's narrative not only echoes Walcott's tale of three family heroes who fight against oppression and for the natural and maternal world. Her narrative, as Giselle Liza Anatol states, also echoes the "numerous allusions to the work firmly insert the novel into a tradition of Caribbean literature that employs folklore to acknowledge and celebrate the native culture: one that has long been denigrated by proponents of European colonialism" ("Soucouyant," 36). Hopkinson's choice to write her novel within this tradition and as a post-apocalyptic dystopian narrative allows her to implicitly portray the destructive period of colonial history as the catastrophic event from which her culture can survive, reject imperial ideology, and from which it may move on and heal. The fact that this survival, rejection, and healing is heralded by a maternal character who carries the next generation in her arms as she does so, is a significant innovative portrayal of dystopian heroism, one made possible by black mothers.

NOTES

1. As evidenced by the burning of Judith Butler in effigy as a "witch" in 2017 in Brazil, among other similar events around the world against "nonconforming" women.

Chapter 4

MATERNAL FUTURES

Maternity and the Holy Book in Parable of the Talents (1999) and Who Fears Death (2014)

In imperial societies throughout history, and particularly in the West, religion and religious texts have been employed to subjugate colonized peoples and justify exploitative treatment of minorities. For example, the *Requerimiento* of 1513, backed by the Catholic Church's interpretation of the Christian *Bible*, justified the forced appropriation of land in the New World and violence against indigenous peoples by the Spanish conquistadors. Manifest Destiny, the idea that white Americans had the God-given right to forcibly claim land from indigenous peoples, was also backed by interpretations of "God's word." Both of these instances of imperial conquest justified by sacred texts are among numerous examples that appear not just in the West, but all over the world, and seem to be part and parcel of any colonial enterprise. When discussing "sacred texts," for the purpose of this monograph I will borrow Paul Gutjahr's definition, which states that "these are sacred books—momentous, spiritual texts that lay claim to special insights . . . call for special levels of allegiance, on account of some form of divine authorship" (335). And because of their presumed special insights and demand of allegiance, the authorship, interpretation, and actions taken on behalf of these books are critical to the underpinning of communities and societies founded on religious belief systems. These formative religions are particularly relevant in the post-apocalyptic landscape, where decimated societies are particularly susceptible to new—or old—ideologies when existing society seems to have crumbled.

In particular, these texts often describe how women—especially mothers—should acceptably function in a society driven by the belief systems buttressed by those texts. The ethnographic study of religious texts reveals how traditional beliefs and practices have changed over time, and because their interpretation is fluid and under constant evolution, the study of the function of women with regard to these texts is a critical means to observe their influence on the patriarchal systems condoned by these texts. As Karen Pechilis states, the

> study of religious women affords us an important opportunity to study change, since religious women are transforming patriarchally defined structures of tradition not only by their presence as women but also through their deliberate engagement of tradition on their own terms; thus they make distinctive contributions to tradition as a *living* entity. (95)

By tracing the influence of religious women, especially those in leadership positions in the religious realm and not just in the past or present, but in visions of the future, we can observe the aspirations of those who seek to figuratively, literally, and literarily rewrite the direction of the traditionally patriarchal and repressive ideologies of their cultures' religious beliefs. Thus, these future women "use tradition to respond rather than conform to religious and cultural expectations," and in doing so, seek to (re)form the role and treatment of women as a whole (Pechilis, 95). This chapter will delve into the ways that women who are mothers to daughters—or daughters of mothers—in a post-apocalyptic environment rewrite sacred texts to conceive a new society in dystopia in the World Fantasy Award-winning novel *Who Fears Death* (2010) by Nnedi Okorafor and Nebula Award-winning novel *Parable of the Talents* (1999) by Octavia Butler. In one novel, a mother establishes a new religion to which her daughter bears witness through her own writing, and in the other, a daughter establishes a new religion through rewriting the story that victimized her mother. By examining relationships between mothers and daughters, this chapter will seek to trace the ways that sacred texts undergo various forms of evolution, from one generation of women to the next, that affect the power structures in which future mothers operate in the post-apocalypse.

In her ambitious essay, "Future Shock: Rewriting the Apocalypse in Contemporary Women's Fiction," Susan Watkins engages in an exhaustive examination of women's apocalyptic writing in the twenty-first century, enumerating the characteristics she has found are shared among the texts by women writers of dystopia and the post-apocalypse. Although these characteristics do not form definitive elements of *all* writing in this genre, they do point to significant interest in portraying particular characteristics of this subgenre of dystopia through a feminine lens. Of the elements Watkins enumerates, there are two characteristics that speak to the placement of Octavia Butler's and Nnedi Okorafor's narratives in the genre of maternal futures that their protagonists carry forward, placing these novels that are centered on forms of motherhood firmly in the growing genre of contemporary women's post-apocalyptic writing. One of these shared elements is centered on "the replacement of colonial and patriarchal narratives of paternity and conquest with metaphors of mother-daughter relationships," which is not simply a replacement of male filial relationships with female ones, but instead reflects an entire restructuring of values and concerns that center on female and maternal concerns in the post-apocalypse (119). Women's post-apocalyptic novels also often center on "an interest in the value and preservation (broadly defined) of literate culture after the destruction" (120). This preservation of, and interest in, writing and book culture is apparent in several novels examined in this monograph, including *Book of the Unnamed Midwife*, *Future Home of the Living God*, and the two novels that form the case studies of this chapter. The reason for this particular interest, which is not often observed in other post-apocalyptic novels is, in part, due to a concern for forming a renewed culture that is based on a tangible and material source for reconceived social structure not centered on ideas of the patriarchal symbolic order. The post-catastrophe can be seen as an opportunity to "rewrite" woman's place in the social order, and writing and literacy form the means of reifying this reimagined society. By incorporating these elements of maternal, feminine, and feminist visions of the post-apocalypse, Butler and Okorafor destabilize the conventional technological and patriarchal assumptions of this genre, and re-form the dystopian genre with a new lens through which to view the post-apocalyptic narratives.

In numerous examples of feminist or femino-centric apocalyptic novels, the narratives center on what Watkins refers to as the "maternal imaginary," in which mother-daughter relationships are central to the narrative, and portray a "positive sense of living in harmony with the natural world [that] is seen as a maternal and generational gift given by one woman to another" (126). The portrayal of these relationships as "positive" and "harmonious" overlooks the profound and realistic conflicts in which these characters engage. In fact, the portions of Butler's novel that are told in the protagonist's daughter's voice are replete with resentment and reproach, likely based on the fact that her mother, the founder of the Earthseed religious community, did not attempt to seek her out after she was kidnapped. Nevertheless, these mother-daughter relationships are central to the rewriting of post-apocalyptic community, and through their writing, the protagonists' daughters are critical in continuing the work of their mothers—including all of their female forebears, not simply their immediate biological mothers—in furthering humanity's progression in devastated dystopian landscapes.

The novel *Who Fears Death?* (2010) is centered on the relationship between Onyesonwu and her mother, Najeeba. From the time that Najeeba learns she is pregnant, she is determined to give birth to and care for the baby, despite the fact that the child is a result of rape and that she must raise the abhorred mixed-race child in exile in the desert. Part of the reason for this self-imposed exile is that the child will be born of mixed ethnicities—in part Najeeba's ethnicity, Okeke, and in part the ethnicity of the rapist, Nuru. This mix of ethnicities results in a child referred to as Ewu. Unlike the daughters in Nalo Hopkinson's novel *Brown Girl in the Ring* (1999), a post-apocalyptic novel also centered on a magically powerful woman who inherits her magical abilities from her mother and grandmother, Okorafor's novel centers on a girl, Onyesonwu, who inherits her magical abilities from her father—a powerful sorcerer whose rape is a forcible attempt to beget a son to fulfill the Great Book's prophecy. Onyesonwu finds, as she grows older, that she has supernatural abilities, and these powers grow stronger as time passes. For the first six years of Onyesonwu's life, the mother and daughter live together isolated in the desert until they find a community in which to settle. Yet the only time the reader sees these two women in conflict is the day after Onyesonwu has voluntarily succumbed to circumcision. Najeeba is horrified that her daughter has undergone this act of female mutilation, but Onyesonwu insists that she wanted to remove the shame that her skin color brings to her mother. This conflict later brings the characters closer together, despite being centered on the *un*-feminist act of female circumcision and internalized patriarchal values, a practice that, as the novel describes, is portrayed to young women as a cleansing ritual. As the narrative progresses, the plot reveals that Najeeba's violation was a form of weaponized rape, a method of subjugation of the Okeke that is promoted in the Great Book. The Great Book is the sacred text of the Nuru and Okeke peoples, and promotes the idea of oppression of the Okeke by the Nuru due to a period in which the Okeke rose above their social status to the apparent harm of both ethnic groups. Onyesonwu is destined to become a post-apocalyptic culture hero by changing the words of the Great Book, and in rewriting them she saves her people from genocide and continued abuse and oppression.

Octavia Butler's novel is also centered, in part, on the relationship between a mother, Lauren Oya Olamina, and her daughter, Larkin. Butler's novel *Parable of the Talents* (1999) is a sequel to the novel *Parable of the Sower*, which focuses on Oya's life and what led her to conceive Earthseed. The novel, *Talents*, takes place in the future year 2032 after Oya has lost her entire family and her home, but has nonetheless established a small community called Acorn that is formed according to the values of her religion, Earthseed. This community exists in the United States after an apocalyptic "Pox" that was caused by "coinciding climatic, economic, and sociological crises" which were devastating:

> The Pox has had the effect of an installment-plan World War III . . . there were several small, bloody shooting wars going on around the world during the

Pox.... [L]eaders knew that they could depend on fear, suspicion, hatred, need, and greed to arouse patriotic support for war. Amid all of this, somehow, the United States of America suffered a major nonmilitary defeat.... What is left of it now, what it has become, I do not know. (Butler, 4)

These words were written by Oya's spouse, Franklin Bankole, who wrote only at the behest of Oya, who "managed to badger him into writing a little" (xiv). In the wake of this terrible and violent apocalypse, a fascist politician rises to power who promotes the aphorism "make America great again," and his repressive policies based on this aphorism cause numerous displaced, oppressed, and traumatized persons, most often minorities, to seek out Earthseed as a refuge. The growing religious colony attracts the attention of the oppressive president and his followers, who seeks to stamp out Earthseed by violent repression through abuse, enslavement, and rape. The narrative is largely told by Larkin, also called Asha Vere, Oya's daughter, who tries to reconcile her mother's religious fervor and passionate concern for the oppressed with what she views as her mother's absence and disregard. Both mother's and daughter's writings mesh in order to form the novel and reify Earthseed as new post-apocalyptic culture.

Both of these novels are driven by mother-daughter interactions, their writings, and their focus on book culture as forming the core of religious practice and values. Rewriting the diegetic sacred text is critical for establishing a new society where the maternal is ennobled rather than oppressed, and where pregnancy can be supported rather than constituting the means by which women may be exploited by patriarchy run amok. The novels, examined together, form a dialogic re-visioning of the future for the maternal in the post-apocalypse.

COUNTERGENEALOGIES AND RELIGIOUS LITERACY AS THE ROAD TO A MATERNAL FUTURE

One of the most critical elements of the new post-apocalyptic world in each of these novels is the fact that each is centered on a burgeoning new religious order, which will prove to be enormously significant in establishing a new society in the post-apocalypse since often religious belief becomes entwined with the formation of national identity. In Butler's novel the protagonist, Oya, is working to establish the Earthseed religion based on the writings of *Earthseed: The Books of the Living* within the Acorn community. In Okorafor's novel, Onyesonwu works to strengthen and hone her supernatural abilities so that she can rewrite the highly influential religious text, the Great Book. The existence of each of these new religious orders is contingent on the writings—or rewritings—of each of the central sacred texts that will reconceive humanity's purpose and the treatment of its members—especially women and mothers—in their post-patriarchal societies. By establishing these new religious paths, these women also seek to establish new national identities and new ways of seeing the maternal.

Octavia Butler's novel purposefully positions itself as the rewriting of a sacred text. The title of the novel is taken from one of the gospels of Jesus that appears in the Christian *Bible*, in which a master leaves a portion of his wealth, a number of talents, in the hands of his servants in order to turn a profit. Two of the servants are praised as being "faithful" by turning a profit on the wealth that is left to them. The third servant, who only protected the wealth and did not turn a profit, was punished. There are numerous interpretations of this tale, as is true of all parables and biblical stories, but it is clear that the master of these servants expected those servants to labor on his behalf so that the master would subsequently profit from this unpaid and uncompensated arrangement. Because the third servant did not participate in this exploitation, he is admonished. Butler's novel obliquely rewrites this story by centering on a mother who establishes a new religion based not on an oppressive and exploitative hierarchy, but instead on equitable authority among all members centered on a reconception of divinity: "God is Change." When the narrator, Oya, remembers her father's telling of this parable, the parable's conclusion immediately merges with her own past trauma, and Oya envisions the sudden disappearance of first her mother, then her father, then her brothers, her entire family, and then her home. Her own body then disappears, and she awakens from what was a nightmare of bodies mysteriously lost. In order to recover from the immense suffering of her past, including the death of most of her family, Oya learns to embrace change, ultimately deifying change itself, and preaching this new religious perspective to others who have suffered almost unimaginable trauma. Oya is also afflicted with a condition called "hyperempathy" that causes her to feel the emotions of others deeply. Her followers have suffered tragedies and traumas of their own, and her hyperempathy allows Oya to understand what her followers need, and as such her religion teaches acute and meaningful ways to alleviate this pain. If change is central to the religion, its texts, and deity worship, and the embrace of change brings comfort to her followers, then it follows that a religion founded by a mother through a transformation of the "standard" religion in the novel—Christianity—is tasked with upending the Judeo-Christian patriarchal culture and transforming the faith community into one that is formed by freedom and equity for its members, and where "the religious language in the novels roots itself in the voice of a female leader concerned about the liberation of women and men alike" (Ruffin, 89).

The first line of the novel's Prologue, after the epigraph, deifies the central character Lauren Oya Olamina, reinforcing her importance to the religion that seeks to survive and surpass the chaotic post-apocalyptic landscape: "They'll make a god of her" (xiii). These words are written by Oya's daughter, Larkin Olamina, who is writing a book about her mother in spite of her animosity:

> I've hated her, feared her, needed her . . . I still don't understand. . . . But I must try because I need to understand myself, and she is part of me. . . . In order for me to understand who I am, I must begin to understand who she was. That is my reason for writing and assembling this book. (xiv)

The relationship between this estranged daughter and her faith-leader mother is a complex one, but Oya's daughter is integral to the perpetuation and maturation of Earthseed: "'God is Change,' my mother believed. That was what she said in the first of her verses in *Earthseed: The First Book of the Living*. . . . And now she's touched me one last time with her memories, her life, and her damned Earthseed" (xv). Her writings, alongside her mother's posthumous sacred texts, establish the maternal foundations of the post-apocalyptic religious order that does not disappear with its founder's death.

The establishment of a new religious understanding occurs in quite a different way in Okorafor's novel. Like Butler's novel, the sacred text has already been written, but although the Christian parable in the novel's title has little to do with the protagonist's Earthseed religion, for the characters in Okorafor's novel the original sacred text is a significant element of the narrative, and provides the impetus for the conception of the religious leader herself—Onyesonwu. The sacred text, simply called the Great Book in Okorafor's novel, describes the violence and racism that occurs between the Nuru, a light-skinned people from west Africa (referred to as "the West,") and the Okeke, dark-skinned and populating west and east Africa. The Great Book calls for the Nuru's oppression of the Okeke, since they are "inferior" and because the Okeke dared to rebel against the book's oppressive hierarchical social arrangement. The Great Book tells of a time when the Okeke revolted against the Nuru, an event that brought about terrible harm for all. As a result of the Great Book's story and the "lesson" implied in the terror of the Okeke uprising, the Nuru must now carry the "burden" of the necessity of violently oppressing the Okeke so that they remain subdued. The Nuru thus commit massacres and weaponized rape in order to impregnate Okeke women with Ewu—children of mixed race who will be maligned and cursed in the Okeke communities. This is a punishment against women, and this is how Najeeba, the protagonist's mother, is impregnated when she is assaulted by Daib, a powerful Nuru sorcerer. Najeeba gives birth to her daughter alone in the desert, and together they wander the wasted landscape until they come upon a community that is willing to tolerate an Ewu child in their midst. This child grows up having learned about her biological father's crime, and vows to hunt him down and defeat him one day, since she has inherited his power and seems to have grown even more powerful as she ages. Her objective is imbued with urgency, since Daib is on a campaign to wipe out the Okeke from "the West" for good—and he expects his male heir to assist him. He is emboldened by the fact that prophets and seers of the Great Book declare that "a Nuru sorcerer would come and change what was written" (Okorafor, 150). In this patriarchal religion, no one suspects that this mixed-race Nuru-Okeke sorceror would in fact be a sorcer*ess*, the female Onyesonwu.

There are elements of the Igbo religion that are apparent throughout the novel. This religion, Odinala, is not referred to specifically in the novel, but Odinala deities such as Ani appear in the narrative, although in numerous imaginative guises. Ani, or Ala, is a chthonic mother deity, or Alusi, who is the mother of all things, including creativity and social order, and she watches over women and children in particular (Ojaide, 44). Ani is present at a human's conception, gestation, and death. She also creates and enforces moral order, ensuring the respect of all human beings for each other. However, her portrayal in the Great Book undermines this understanding of the goddess. In the Great Book, she is arbitrary, declaring one ethnicity superior over another, and justifies violence. This depiction is quite unlike the goddess as she is largely recognized and worshiped, and this disruption and misinterpretation are purposeful on the part of the author. Okorafor is underscoring the danger of sacred books that purposefully misinterpret religious beliefs for the dangerous and xenophobic purposes of the sacred text's writer. In a scene in the novel, a traveling storyteller visits the village where Onyesonwu lives, and tells stories from the Great Book, including the first story that appears in the sacred text. The story describes the goddess Ani's creation of the Okeke people, who invented technology and innovated their society and industry in many different ways. But this technological and social progress is blamed for the apocalyptic event that has left the land in the state that it is in—by purportedly angering the goddess. Thus, Ani plucked the Nuru people from the sun, and cursed the Okeke with the word "slave," and now the "Nuru to this day point at the Okeke and say, *slave* and the Okeke must bow their heads in agreement" (92–93). After recounting this post-apocalyptic and xenophobic re-visioning of the traditional understanding of the goddess, the storyteller goes on to describe the Nuru abuse of her mother: "Nuru men raped my mother repeatedly. They wanted to make an *Ewu* child . . . my mother's mind cracked and the stories she carried spilled out. . . . When they finished, they took my mother. I never saw her again" (93). The story of her mother is the storyteller's cautionary tale—because of the Great Book's disjointed account of Ani, the Nuru raped and kidnapped her mother, and even the eastern town of Jwahir is not safe from an impending Nuru attack. An Okeke member of the audience justifies the attack because "it's been written in the Great Book," and the storyteller responds by asking, "Written by who?" Onyesonwu realizes that the storyteller had "only been telling the *story* of our so-called creation. She didn't believe it" (94). Thus, although many—mostly men—believe and have internalized the Great Book's portrayal of the goddess, there is—mostly among women—an undercurrent of disbelief and questioning of who in fact imagined and wrote down the story. This scene of storytelling and disbelief underscores the necessity and urgency that the Great Book must be rewritten.

In both of these novels, mothers take the reins of changing the increasingly retrograde patriarchal religious beliefs of their respective post-apocalyptic cultures and societies, and because they are women, their efforts are not only repressed but derided, and these women are accused of shameful behavior out of bounds with what is considered proper for women. In her religious community named Acorn, Oya is derided and threatened by the media and by a group called Church of Christian America as maintaining a non-Christian and (thus) immoral commune. In her attempts to become a trained sorcerer, Onyesonwu is derided as being "only a woman" and thus unfit to train and join the ranks of religious leaders such as Aro and Ssaiku. Yet, mother and daughter are assisted in unexpected ways by their daughter and mother, and these generations of women establish a lineage that sets the stage for an empowered maternal future.

Despite the consistent vilification she and her followers suffer at the hands of the fascist president and his followers, the Christian American Crusaders, Oya persists in her attempts to promote a religion that defies their patriarchally motivated abuses. The Christian America Crusaders group has been given implicit sanction by the U.S. president to occupy communities such as Acorn, enslave their inhabitants, rape the women, and enforce ultraconservative and retrogressive laws. While the Crusaders occupy the Acorn community, the women are told "You don't speak unless you're spoken to. . . . It's time for you to learn to behave like decent Christian women—if you've got the brains to learn" (200). When Oya and the other community members finally escape their imprisonment by the Crusaders, Oya seeks out her brother, who has eagerly joined the Christian America group, although he denies that the group would commit the abuses Oya describes. Instead of consoling his sister or helping Oya locate her daughter, Marcus, as a minister for Christian America, instead admonishes her and then, as Oya describes, "He hit me. . . . Even when we were kids, he and I didn't hit each other. . . . And he was gone" (313). The description of this extremist group is remarkably prescient, as it describes not only the leanings of the U.S.

president Donald Trump, who remained in power from 2017 to 2021, but also his followers, whose extremist views of

> the current form of globalism—multiculturalism, inclusion of minorities, universal human rights, erasure of national boundaries—is not the same as it was in the interwar period, [but] the revolt against it looks eerily similar to the rise of European fascism. (Biale, 142)

The seemingly sudden state-sanctioned retrogression of equal rights for women, and their retrogression to degenerate status, is a surprise to Oya and the other women in the Acorn community, in spite of the abuses they have endured in the past. Even after escaping from the Crusaders' occupation of her community, Oya persists in expanding her religion and its texts. Perhaps by continuing to promote the idea of Earthseed among any and all potential followers, and ultimately setting the stage for her followers' eventual sacred Destiny on other planets, Oya provides a means to protect her kidnapped daughter from the growing oppression and repression of women in the post-apocalyptic era, in spite of the fact that her daughter is absent, and in spite of her daughter's later textual misgivings.

Okorafor's novel, however, is told almost entirely from the perspective of Onyesonwu, placing the narrative action at a distance from the protagonist's mother, relative to the mother and daughter textual intimacy of Butler's novel. Yet both mother and daughter, like the mother and daughter who are central to Butler's novel, are subject to an intensely patriarchal religious belief system, although Onyesonwu and her mother, Najeeba, are surrounded by a patriarchal *culture* as well. The sexism is apparent, for example, when Onyesonwu attempts to receive mystical religious and magical training from the only available teacher, Aro, and he rejects her, stating that "You're female. You can't measure up" (Okorafor, 66). This accusation is echoed by Onyesonwu's friend and lover, Mwita, who blames her for the teacher's rejection. Although Mwita continues to make occasional sexist remarks directed at Onyesonwu, he is empathetic to other maternal characters, and sometimes even "checked pregnant women's bellies to make sure all was well" (341). Nevertheless, Mwita is an exception as patriarchal values are written in the Great Book's stories and promoted by most male characters, just as patriarchal values are written into the Bible that Marcus follows. The Great Book describes not only the oppression upon the Okeke due to the supposed ethnic superiority of the Nuru but also the entitlement of the Nuru to commit weaponized rape. This acceptance of Nuru violent oppression upon the Okeke is internalized by both ethnicities. During a public storytelling gathering, an Okeke man declares, "It's been written in the Great Book. We are what we are. We shouldn't have risen up on the first place! Let those who did die for it!" Onyesonwu inwardly responds to the Book's adherents, thinking to herself: "What did this man think of . . . me? That we somehow deserved what we got? . . . That my mother deserved rape?" (94). Similar to the response to the outrages of rape and abuse suffered by Oya, whose writings defy the oppression of patriarchal followers of the sacred text of the Christian American Crusaders, Onyesonwu is determined to rewrite the Great Book by defeating her father, who is a paradigm of the patriarchal oppression of her people. Unfortunately, she must confront the internalized racism and sexism of her own people, who have accepted the beliefs of the Book, in addition to the abuses of the Nuru, and turn their own frustrations upon the Ewu mixed-race persons in their midst.

Like Larkin, who spends much of the novel coming to terms with her discovery of her mother's identity and her religion, Onyesonwu spends much of the novel interacting with her mother in a conventional way, but discovers that her mother is far more powerful than she ever revealed to her daughter. Onyesonwu has the supernatural ability to shape-shift, which allows her to travel quickly and unnoticed by most human beings in her vicinity. Her lover, Mwita, student of the great Aro, explains this unusual ability to Onyesonwu, telling her "you have the ability to *alu*," a word that comes from the Alusi, or spirits worshiped in the Igbo religion. Onyesonwu asks Mwita how he can possibly know this about her, and he reveals that Onyesonwu's mother, Najeeba, is close to Ada, or "the Ada," a magical practitioner married to the great Aro, who has taught both Mwita and Onyesonwu his magical practice. Mwita says that

> this is how I know about your mother. . . . Your mother knew exactly what she was doing when she asked that you be a sorceress once you were born and a girl. It was her revenge. . . . Your mother can travel within, she can *alu*. (308)

Mwita reveals that Onyesonwu's mother was aware that she had supernatural abilities, to such a degree that "even Aro looked envious when he told me about the many places [Onyesonwu's] mother has traveled" (310). In the novel's third chapter, Najeeba recounts how she wants to die after she has been raped, and lies in the desert hoping for death by exposure, but since she was raped by a powerful magical practitioner, she realized her progeny would be born with power that may surpass both of her parents. If that child would be born a girl, then that girl may be able to take revenge on not just the man who raped her, but on all of the men who systematically rape the Okeke. Thus Najeeba chooses to live and carry the baby to term, and thus her naming, Onyesonwu, which means "Who fears death?" Certainly not this powerful offspring. Najeeba silently supports her daughter, both empathetically and magically, but her choice for her daughter's name may be her earliest gift, since Onyesonwu derives strength from her name to reify her resolve: "I willed it, as I repeated my name in my mind like a mantra" (334).

Mwita continues to reveal that Najeeba's power is so significant that

> your mother would have passed initiation. This is what Aro believes after talking to both your mother and the Ada. It has something to do with your grandmother.... There is always this energy between your kind.... It's part of why you and your mother are so close. And it's probably why Daib chose your mother to impregnate. Your mother can become two beings, herself and an Alusi—she can split herself. (309)

Aro thus believes that this supernatural ability is passed on maternally—from grandmother, to mother, to daughter. This maternal legacy is one that materially undermines the entire underpinning of the Great Book and its belittling portrayal of women and motherhood. Najeeba was not a passive victim; she reappraises the terrible trauma and exploitation she has experienced to ensure that the powerful maternal legacy of supernatural abilities continues through her daughter. Mwita goes on to explain that Onyesonwu's

> mother's mother, Sa'eeda, was also a free spirit. And though she loved her children, motherhood was not easy for her... I closed my eyes as Mwita told me these things that my mother had told the Ada and never told me. (310)

This description of the maternal lineage describes women who are alike not only in their possession of the Alu shape-shifting and traveling ability but also in their personality and beliefs—that they are free spirited and unhindered by patriarchal oppression, shame, or accusations of impropriety.

Once Onyesonwu has finally learned of this incredible maternal legacy, she understands the incredible empathy that Najeeba has demonstrated when the unexpected manifestation of her daughter's powers caused Onyesonwu to transform uncontrollably in crowded areas and public events. The empathy originates from the fact that Najeeba herself has this ability. Najeeba empathizes with her daughter's inability to control or understand what was happening to her when she would wake to find herself flying in the form of a bird, for example. Onyesonwu feels some resentment that her mother didn't tell her about this inheritance earlier, thinking

> I wish it was my mother who told me what Mwita went on to tell me. I'd have loved to hear it from her. But my mother has always been full of secrets. It was that Alusi side, I guess. (309)

This resentment does not remain, as the dwindling group travels onward and realizes Onyesonwu's mother is doing what she can to help them by spreading the word that the Okeke's savior is on her way. The farther west Onyesonwu, Mwita, and Luyu travel, the more danger they are in—unless they have the support of the Okeke. Outside of a village called Gadi, the three friends reflect on what they have recently overheard: "They said an Okeke woman who never ate but looked well fed has been going around 'whispering the news.... She predicts an *Ewu* sorceress will end their suffering'" (341). This magical woman is preceding Onyesonwu, protecting her by preparing the populace for her arrival: "My mother! ... My mother was going *alu*, sending herself here and telling the Okeke about me, to expect me and be glad. Aro truly was teaching her, then" (341). This effort reveals the *combined* effort of mother and daughter will allow for the Great Book to be rewritten by paving the way for her acceptance. The Okeke mistrust anyone of Ewu descent, and would likely react violently to Onyesonwu if not for her mother's intervention.

Onyesonwu not only maintains a connection with her mother through Najeeba's protective intercession, but she also maintains a connection with her lover through the site of her own maternal future—her uterus. When she is unable to find her lover Mwita, she is able to connect to him by communing with her uterus where his sperm is housed, the morning after they have sex:

> I need to find Mwita ... *I can find Mwita*, I realized. I had a part of him in me. His sperm. Connection. I stood very still and turned inward. Through my skin, fat, muscle, into my womb. There they were, wriggling away. "Where is he?" I asked. They told me. (359)

Onyesonwu's womb causes her distress during their journeys, and she occasionally complains, such as when "my monthly made my womb hot as a rock fire stone," but her womb is, for her, simultaneously a source of knowledge and insight (312). This physiological link between Onyesonwu, her mother Najeeba, and her grandmother Sa'eeda, and all other mothers and potential mothers, functions as a significant source of power for these maternal characters in the novel, and one that they draw on as they progress in defeating Daib and rewriting the Great Book.

This connection with her uterus reaches a critical juncture when her lover and father of her future children dies without impregnating her. This trauma sends Onyesonwu into an apotheosis, and she screams for her mother: "'Mama!' I screamed ... 'Mama, help me!' ... 'Mama!'" (367). Onyesonwu depends on her mother's empathy, assistance, and wisdom, and when she calms for a moment, she turns to her womb for guidance and power:

> As I held Mwita's body, a thought occurred to me. I ... immediately acted on it ... Mwita and I had not slept last night.... He was still inside me. He was still

alive. I felt them in me, swimming, wriggling. I was not at my moon's peak but I made it so. I moved my egg to meet what I could find of Mwita's life. . . . At the moment of conception, a giant shock wave blasted from me, a shock wave like the one so long ago during my father's burial ceremony. It blew out the walls around me and the ceiling above me. (367–368)

This self-directed impregnation proves more decisive for Onyesonwu's maternal journey than her ultimate defeat of her biological father, Daib. And the destruction that this obliquely parthenogenetic act engenders is related to the first manifestations of her power, suggesting that *all* of her power emanates from her uterus. This empowerment as proceeding from the female reproductive system is not isolated to Onyesonwu. As Onyesonwu recalls: "I thought of the female [magic] apprentice Sanchi, who'd obliterated an entire town when she conceived as a student. I thought of Aro's reservations about training girls and women" (368). Thus, as Aro is aware, women have an exclusive destructive power that emanates from their wombs. This also suggests that as Najeeba lay dying in the desert, after being raped by Daib, she could have brought about her own pregnancy, since as a magical being she would have been able to direct her uterus to bring about the conception of Onyesonwu. The power and ability to conceive at will allows these women to control both their maternal path and the direction of humankind in the post-apocalypse—and will allow them to reconceive how their religion and culture will perceive women and maternity in its future.

Although she is not supernaturally empowered by her womb as Onyesonwu is, Oya's motivations to find her daughter drive many of her actions in the novel. Both novels hinge on the interdependence of mothers and daughters, whether or not these women feel affection or resentment for each other. Each of these women depends on the other for empowerment and identity, and mothers support their daughters in bringing about a new spiritual or religious awareness. This awareness is critical for the instantiation and rewriting of the sacred texts that are central to their religious practice and future nation-building.

MOTHERS, DAUGHTERS, AND (RE) WRITING THE NEW ORDER

When considering the history of the printed word, innovations in writing are often intertwined with religious practice. In China, one of the countries from which the earliest fonts of written language emerged, writing likely flourished alongside religious practice, as Adam Yuet Chau argues:

> This religious practice is the 'cherishing of written characters' . . . which involves the reverence for the written word, especially the peculiar practice of picking up any scrap paper with any writing on it . . . and burning it respectfully in . . . a temple dedicated to . . . the patron deity of the traditional literati. (118)

Early Egyptian writings appeared in temples and tombs, where sacred stories of the gods are depicted. In the West, the Gutenberg printing press is known for the first printed book, the Bible. In addition to these, there are numerous examples of writing and literacy "firsts" that have developed alongside or in tandem with a religion's texts. These innovations were both formed and framed by significant cultural transitions. The same may be said for the apocalyptic events portrayed in Butler's and Okorafor's novels, and the religious texts that manifest after the catastrophe.

Beyond the protagonists' religious development and associated writings, these women's relationships with their mothers contribute to their progression as religious leaders and authors. The careful preservation of her mother's writing and its integration in her own book point to the maternal generation of a new bond between Larkin and her mother Oya, formed through writing in the post-apocalyptic context. Despite her animosity toward her mother, Larkin finds that she and her mother share a significant creative and communicative outlet: "It has always been my way to sort through my feelings by writing. She and I had that in common" (Butler, xiv). Larkin has preserved her mother's work, admitting that "I have copies of all that was saved of her writings. Even some of her early, paper notebooks have been copied to disk or crystal and saved" (xiv). By preserving these writings, Larkin also preserves the literacy and foundational text that contributes to an expansion of Earthseed in the future.

In *Parable of the Talents*, Larkin's preservation of her mother's writing and its integration in her own book point to the maternal generation of new sacred texts in the post-apocalyptic milieu. The preservation of her writing, and her mother's, is critical to (re)forming their religious community in the post-apocalypse context. By centering her writing within her mother's journal entries, Larkin inserts her own reflections within the written episodes of her mother's life, retelling her mother's experiences in the framework of her own. Karen Pechilis states that the act of storytelling contributes to women's entrance into the vocation of faith leadership, because "engag[ing] in the praxis of religious storytelling, through which their religious authority is both articulated and asserted . . . demonstrates their religious expertise (knowledge) but also contributes to the production of their prestige (influence) as leaders" (97). Persistent storytelling based on personal hardship infuses each of these women with distinction, which is necessary in order to combat the assumptions and presumptions they are faced with within a civilization in decline. This religious influence is reinforced when these women's stories reflect their own life experiences, because

> there is a reflexivity insofar as the biographies become descriptive of the teller's religiosity and constitutive of her devotion and authority . . . [when she] tells stories that are explicitly autobiographical . . . as both describing and validating her power. (Pechilis, 97)

Oya's sacred texts are written alongside the early diary entries of her personal experiences, making them inherently autobiographical. Their transformation through her daughter's retelling form foundational texts for her religious order and enacts a form of canonization—by means of her deification and in the reading of her journals as texts. Thus, telling stories about each other—through each other—within the context of religious formation reinforces the command that these women—mother and daughter—have over the new community they are constructing in the post-apocalypse.

One of the journal entries describes the affect elicited by Oya's sacred text. In the period after the Acorn community has been destroyed and her daughter kidnapped, Oya wanders on her own, in search of information that may reveal where her daughter is being held. As she travels, and in spite of all that she has lost, Oya maintains her faith in Earthseed, and believes that she must find a new way to reassemble and perpetuate her religious community: "I sit here now, trying to think, to plan. I must find my daughter, and I must teach Earthseed, make Earthseed real to as many people as I can reach, and send them out to teach others" (293). As she renews her efforts to proselytize, her writings are formative in instilling the concepts of her sacred text in the minds of those she encounters, which are equally as powerful as the predominant Christian sacred text:

> Some people even seemed to think that what I read was from the Bible. I couldn't bring myself to let them go on thinking that . . . . "It's from something else called *Earthseed: The Books of the Living*." And I showed them one of the few surviving copies. . . . In that way, I guess I never stopped teaching Earthseed. (293–294)

These are the first few steps Oya takes in forming a larger religious practice, one that has a better chance of spreading and becoming permanent if she discovers those who may be not only agreeable to learn but will pass on this information didactically:

> I must find at least a few people who are willing to learn more, and who will be willing to teach . . . I need to create something wide-reaching and harder to kill

... I must create not only a dedicated little group of followers, not only a collection of communities as I once imagined but a movement ... that can evolve into a new religion, a new guiding force. (295)

If Earthseed resided only in Acorn, then the fascist president Jarrett would have quashed the religion with the invasion of his Crusaders. But Oya's religion is in the beginning stages of a movement, unbreakable and self-perpetuating, and safeguarded by her daughter.

Onyesonwu, on the other hand, is not attempting to instantiate a new religious practice, but instead hopes to elicit help and training so that she may strengthen her latent supernatural powers, defeat her biological father, and then rewrite the Great Book. Although women are not the only characters to learn about the power of writing and book culture, the most powerful and visible women in both novels do turn to writing and literacy as a means of empowerment. Women, religious practice, and writing are critical for the magical teachings that Onyesonwu hopes to learn. During her travels, she meets a woman named Ting who is also a sorcerer. Ting's body is marked with a number of symbols, and she reveals to Onyesonwu that they are not simply decorative, but are characters of a magical language. She tells Onyesonwu that "writing scripts are my center ... What I'm most gifted at ... I can't tell you exactly what my markings mean, not in words. They changed my life, each in their own needed way" (261). Ting, Onyesonwu, Nana the Wise, all are powerful women who have mastered writing as a source of, and tool for, their empowerment and for religious transformation.

However, these women must hone their abilities in spite of the violence perpetrated by men who seek to discourage their progress, or who oppress them to the point that they internalize the belief that they are incapable. Although Aro, a stalwart sorcerer and teacher, initially rejects Onyesonwu because she is female, she seeks out help on her own while continuing to persistently plead with Aro to teach her. He finally acquiesces, and Onyesonwu's eyes are opened to the larger realm of magic and its possibilities. Empowered and confident, she later travels to the West to find and confront her biological father, Daib, the powerful sorcerer and general who is at the cusp of launching a deadly attack against the Okeke to decisively remove them from the West once and for all. Onyesonwu travels alongside her lover, Mwita, and her friends Luyu, Diti, and Binta. During her travels, she learns that her reputation as a sorcerer has preceded her (thanks to her mother), and that she has already solidified the foundation of her religious authority—she has become a source of hope for the Okeke fighters. In order to gain information on Daib's whereabouts, Luyu decides to approach a group of Okeke fighters, and her friends direct her to "tell them that you, bring good news of the coming of Onyesonwu, something like that," and Luyu does so, saying:

> "I bring you good news. . . . Have you heard of the Sorcerer Onyesonwu?"
> "I have," the head soldier said with a nod.
> "She's here with me. . . . Will you harm us?" Luyu asked.
> He looked Luyu in the eye. "No." His restraint broke and a tear fell from his eye.
> "We'd *never* harm you." (348–349)

But despite the faith and hope that has been built around her, especially with the help of her mother, Onyesonwu is nonetheless subject to paternalistic or sexist jokes. When Mwita tells the soldier that they had been traveling for about five months, the soldier says "I applaud you. . . . All this way, leading two women at that" (349). Although Onyesonwu may be a powerful savior and source of hope, she is nonetheless "only a woman."

One aspect of rewriting the Great Book isn't simply reframing its overall narrative with regard to the Nuru and Okeke, but in critiquing and reimagining the shorter stories that make up the larger whole. One of these stories is diegetically well-known and influential, but is one that is so hated by Onyesonwu that she recounts the parable with disgust, and the lessons that children should learn from its telling are preceded by "meant to" and "supposed to," reinforcing the farcical quality of the tale, in her view: "In the Great Book, their story was one of triumph and sacrifice. . . . It's supposed to remind you that great things will always be protected. . . . It's all a lie" (242). The tale is centered on patriarchy that seems to have run amok, except for the fact that the events it portrays are so similar to nondiegetic ancient parables. The story purports to center on the male characters—the successive chiefs of a place called Suntown, but in fact hinges on the maternal—the impregnation of women, the timing of births, and a critical midwife whose actions foreground the patriarchal lessons the listener is supposed to learn. The story is about Tia and Zoubeir. Tia's birth was "nothing special," and was welcomed because "the first child had been a healthy boy" (242). Zoubeir's conception occurred because a chief who possessed four wives already, noticed a woman at a party and he

> sought her out and had her over and over until she became pregnant. Then he told his soldiers to kill her. There was a rule . . . the first son born out of wedlock to the chief must succeed him. The chief's father had avoided this rule by marrying every woman he bedded . . . he had over three hundred wives. (242–243)

The issue of consent is never mentioned, but the implication is that these sexual encounters are rape, and each marriage is made under coercion. Clearly, the potential birth of an heir out of the chief's control is unacceptable for the chief and his father. By marrying each woman, each chief keeps all births within his control, and is not compelled to consider his own mortality (by being faced with his replacement) or the consequences of impregnating so many women. Each of these women, though, is unable to have a family of her own, a love interest of her choosing, and in many ways is ostracized from her family and her own agency. In the case of "the chief" and "the woman," she must be killed to remove any chance of birthing a threat to his dominion. However, "this woman was three months pregnant when she outran the soldiers sent to kill her. Eventually . . . she gave birth to a son she named Zoubeir" (243). This period, at the end of the first trimester of most regular pregnancies, is a time when the gravida begins to feel the weight of the unborn child, and when regular movements begin to become a challenge. This woman lives on to raise the future chief, but the incredible feat of being three months pregnant and still outrunning soldiers is an achievement that is given little notice in the tale. The story goes on to state that on

> the day of Zoubeir's and Tia's births, the midwife ran back and forth between their mothers' huts. They were born at the exact same time, but the midwife chose to stay with Zoubeir's mother because she had a feeling that this woman's child was a boy and the other woman's child was a girl. (243)

The magical realism of the tale gives the narrative a magical quality, particularly at this point when the two fateful children are born at the same time. But the midwife's prescience and preference reinforce the patriarchal values and overtones in the narrative, suggesting that escaping the patriarchal value system is impossible since even a midwife embodies those values by making decisions based on them. There is a comparison between the ways that the two children are raised: Zoubeir grows "loud-mouthed," while Tia's "father often beat her . . . and her father began to have eyes for her too. . . . So Tia grew the opposite of Zoubeir, short and silent" (243). Thus, Zoubeir has the freedom to speak his mind and "live out loud," while Tia is silenced, and must also suffer the implied sexual abuse of her father. At the tale's denouement, the now mortally ill chief finds out about his son's existence, and sends his soldiers to kill him, and finding Tia and Zoubeir sitting together under a tree,

> one of them brought his gun up. . . . Then she just knew. *Not him*, she thought . . . throwing herself over him. Of course she caught the bullet and Zoubeir did not . . . as Zoubeir hid behind her body. He pushed her off him and ran. . . . He escaped and went on to become the greatest chief Suntown ever had. (244)

The tale's ending is meant to laud the great Zoubeir, and teach girls that their greatest purpose in life is to sacrifice for a man, even if that means they give up their lives. However, the tale does not glorify Tia's great sacrifice, as Onyesonwu notes:

> He never built a shrine or a temple or even a shack in the name of Tia. In the Great Book, her name is never mentioned again. He never mused about her or even asked where she was buried. . . . And she was a girl. It was her duty to sacrifice her life for his. I've always disliked this story. (244)

Thus, the female character, born at the same moment as the chief, was purposed to die so that the male child could go on to become a great leader, which is an echo of numerous expectations made of female characters throughout the novel. Yet the story's dismissal of its female characters and glorification of the male characters may prompt the reader or listener to ask: Which of these characters truly enacted great feats? Was it the male characters, who inherit their titles as chief and who impregnate as many women as they feel, entitled to impregnate? Or is it the female characters, who outrun soldiers while pregnant, attend to multiple births simultaneously, presage the sex of the infants, and throw their bodies in front of weapons to save the life of another? This story, among others, drives Onyesonwu's determination to rewrite the Great Book.

These parables that appear within the larger narrative of the goddess Ani's cursing of the Okeke highlight the patriarchal undertones of the entirety of the Great Book. But the misogyny and xenophobia perpetuated by these stories will not change until the entire book is understood and rewritten. The apocalyptic event has rendered the pre-catastrophe era a mystery to those living in the diegetic present. The leftover technology from this forgotten era has provided tangible material from which to rewrite the goddess Ani in the Great Book. As Onyesonwu and her friends travel west to confront Daib, they stop in a cave to shelter from a storm. And there, in

> the back of the cave, half covered with sand that had swept in over the years, were possibly hundreds of computers, monitors, portables, and e-books. . . . Old and amazingly ancient things packed in a cave in the middle of nowhere and long forgotten. . . . The Great Book spoke of such places, caves full of computers . . . put here by terrified Okekes trying to escape Ani's wrath . . . just before she brought the Nuru from the stars to enslave the Okeke. . . . Did this mean that parts of the Great Book were true? Had the Okeke really crammed technology away in caves to hide them from an angry goddess?" (329–330)

Without the ability to see her civilization before the catastrophe, Onyesonwu finds it difficult to understand if the story was written based on the discovery of this discarded technology, or if the hardware indeed appeared in the caves as a result of the wrath of a goddess. Onyesonwu and her friends find the technology disturbing for this reason—its possible verification of the sacred text—and avoid the cache of artifacts as much as they can. But Onyesonwu finally decides to approach "the electronics at the back of the cave . . . the old devices of a doomed people" and decided to "look doom in the face" (334–335). As uncomfortable as this confrontation is for her and her friends, Onyesonwu realizes that "this was a page right out of the Great Book. If I was going to somehow rewrite it then it made sense for me to look" (335). Confronting the pre-apocalypse, the "before times," an era when the Okeke were presumably a free people, will provide insight, Onyesonwu hopes, into how she will complete her perplexing mission. While she is peering at the "cursed junk," Onyesonwu notices a book within the rubble. The "book" is, in fact, an e-book, and the screen miraculously lights up when Onyesonwu touches a button. The screen reveals "a place of plants, trees, and bushes. . . . *Just like the place my mother showed me*, I thought. *The place of hope*" (335). Onyesonwu is often reminded of the *locus amoenus* her mother once showed her, and with her arrival in any new region, she makes a comparison of the landscape with this remembered vista. Is this a sign from the goddess? The title of the book suddenly appears: *The Forbidden Greeny Jungle Field Guide*. The message seem clear: the locus amoenus where her hope resides is forbidden, but this garden must remain her goal. Peace resides here, as does prosperity, if only this new story can be written over the old. The authors of field guide are called "The Great Explorers of Knowledge and Adventure Organization," and this organization's name seems to be an invitation for Onyesonwu to join them in their regenerative story.

> But how will Onyesonwu rewrite the sacred text? The idea seems absurd to her, and she asks the magical teacher Oga Sola "So, what am I to do . . . ?" (318). Sola answers,
> "'Rewrite the Great Book . . . Don't you know that?'
> . . . 'But how do I *do* that, Oga Sola? The idea doesn't even make sense! . . . You can't rewrite a book that is already written and known by thousands of people. And it's not even the book that is making people behave this way.'
> 'Are you sure about that?' Sola coldly asked. 'Have you *read* it?'
> 'Of course I have, *Oga*' I said . . . but I felt I needed to look at the book again . . .
> 'Leave the book now. You know what you have to do'" (318).

The Great Book's rewriting will not stem from logic or reason, but from intuition, and will become clear to Onyesonwu once she has defeated Daib. And indeed, when Onyesonwu and Mwita finally reach Daib in the town called Durfa, he tells them,

> Get out of here . . . I have a plan to complete. Rana's prophecy to fulfill—"a tall bearded Nuru sorcerer will come and force the Great Book's rewriting." What a different book it will be once I exterminate the rest of the Okeke. (364)

The sacred text has been re-interpreted yet again, and now Daib sees himself as the author that the prophet Rana the Seer foretold. Like Rudy from the novel *Brown Girl in the Ring* (1998), Daib sees himself as the Übermensch who will control soldiers "like cows" and taking pleasure in abusing women, gloating that "I prefer to bash an Okeke woman's head in after I've had her. Except your mother . . . She should have given me a great, great son. Why are you a girl?" (365). Onyesonwu's abilities and accomplishments are meaningless thus far, because of the fact that she is female. After subduing Mwita, Daib turns to Onyesonwu and declares that he will destroy her body and her spirit, and states "I'll find your mother. She'll bear my son" (366). At this point, Mwita leaps up and adheres a written curse to Daib's neck, one written by the sorceress-scribe Ting. He is then mortally wounded by Daib, but before he dies, he tells Onyesonwu "Find it . . . Finish it," revealing that it is not Onyesonwu's destiny to single-handedly defeat Daib, but instead to rewrite the Great Book, and she must do this by finding the Book's powerful guardian, Rana the Seer (367).

After the confrontation and defeat of the wicked sorcerer, Onyesonwu and Luyu exit Daib's decimated building and notice that the town has changed—for the maternal. Onyesonwu realizes that "every single male human in the central town of Durfa capable of impregnating a woman was dead. My actions had killed them . . . every single one of those men had instantly died" (370). Luyu vomits and complains that she feels ill. Onyesonwu knows why, and reveals to her: "You're pregnant . . . I made myself conceive. Something happened because of it . . . I don't know how far it went. . . . But where there are dead men, there are pregnant women" (371). Along with her auto-conception and subsequent destruction of Daib's center of operations, Onyesonwu has caused men to die and all women in the vicinity to become spontaneously pregnant, bringing about an incredible wave of maternity and maternocentricity to a region where women were suppressed by men—as Daib demanded.

Before her cultural transformation has truly taken hold, Onyesonwu is imprisoned near the novel's conclusion. While detained, she retells her entire story to another woman, a Nuru woman who "thought it was all wrong, the way we lived, behaved, [according to] the Great Book" (380). This Nuru woman, who did not condone the mistreatment of the Okeke, adds that all of the women Onyesonwu saved and impregnated are also given supernatural abilities, including the ability to fly and to remember the world before the apocalyptic Great Book shattered their culture: the future mothers now have "thousands of abilities. All bestowed upon women. . . . In the death of herself and her child, Onye gave birth to us all" (381). In this way, Onyesonwu has not just empowered women, but now maternal women, with supernatural abilities, bringing about a rebirth of how women will be perceived in this new post-apocalyptic society. Onyesonwu admits that she may have acted impulsively, and this is true—these women did not give their consent to become pregnant. Her goal is to, in her view, give women a gift that was taken from her and that she would never experience—to give birth.

Just before her imprisonment, Onyesonwu and Luyu are being chased by the few remaining Nuru men who were standing just outside of the outer reaches of Onyesonwu's magical transformation of Durfa. Onyesonwu runs to reach Rana the Seer's hut, but finding Rana dead, turns to the ancient book calling to her. The Book, she notes, "reminded me of the black cover of the electronic book I found in that cave," thus drawing a connection between the old technology that she "read" and the new one that she would "write." As she holds the book, she intuitively knows how to rewrite the story, and this reconception of the Great Book takes place maternally:

> This book was full of hate and that was what caused its sickness. . . . Then I began to sing . . . the song that I had made up when I was . . . living with my mother in the desert . . . I saw the symbols . . . dribbled down into the book where they settled between the other symbols into a script . . . I could feel the book sucking from me, as a child does from its mother's breast. Taking and taking. I felt something click within my womb. (376–377)

The rewriting of the book, then, occurs through Onyesonwu's maternity, by means of her breasts and her womb, where an embryo has now formed. The maternal metaphor is one of gestation and birthing, as the book takes its nourishment from her body and is reborn at the point when she felt "something click."

The book ends with "Chapter 1: Rewritten," and describes Onyesonwu's newly written narrative where she flies to meet Mwita again. The chapter leaves unclear whether or not Onyesonwu is truly dead, though "her friends had died, her Mwita," but in spite of their passing, "she was *not* a sacrifice . . . for the good of men and women, Okeke and Nuru alike. She was Onyesonwu. She had rewritten the Great Book" (384–385). Nevertheless, she returns to the "green place her mother had shown her . . . where the land was blanketed with leafy trees, bushes, plants. . . . He would be waiting" (385). This locus amoenus is her final destination, and in the final page of the novel, the narrator asks, "what will become of their daughter who laughed so gleefully inside Onyesonwu's belly on the way to the green place?" (386). Perhaps this future daughter, too, will be (re)born and continue the legacy that has been passed down from one mother to another, to carry on rewriting where necessary, and to perhaps function as a steward and storyteller of the rewritten Great Book.

In *Parable of the Talents*, Larkin conducts a form of rewriting and stewardship of her mother's sacred book by interspersing her text with scriptures taken from Oya's *Earthseed: Books of the Living*. The scriptures are quoted piecemeal as epigraphs at the start of each of the novel's chapters. The inclusion of excerpts of her meta-fictional books creates a substantive foundation for her religion's sacred texts in the novel's dystopian universe. Epigraphs are not simply decorative text that precedes the substance of a book's principal content but serves a significant purpose—whether or not the writer who includes those epigraphs is aware of their influence on the rest of the text. The epigraph serves a dialogic purpose, as Megan Thornton states:

> While these peripheral elements are rarely commented on as part of an intertextual dialogue, their presence constructs meaning and inspires thought-provoking interpretations. Epigraphs, quotations placed at the beginning of a text, are particularly important to the study of intertextuality because they identify an author's reading experience as well as her influential predecessors. (151–152)

Thus, the inclusion of excerpts of the meta-fictional *Earthseed: The Books of the Living*, written by Oya, establish the text as an anticipatory foundational source from which epigraphs may be taken—the book is a reified, substantive material text, though it may only be accessed by the reader through the inclusion of epigraphs. The epigraphs form an intertextuality that is centered on a sacred future writing that doesn't yet exist and that a priori establishes a religion's core text before it has been written, and founds the post-apocalyptic faith community in anticipation of the apocalypse.

The epigraphs further point to the necessity of rethinking human religious community in the post-apocalypse. The central tenet of Earthseed is "God is Change," but the brief epigraphs delve deeper into the transitional nature of pre- and post-apocalypse, in addition to the evolution of religion as a result of the cataclysm. The excerpts from the sacred texts repeatedly encourage followers to look inward for guidance, a "heretical" form of religious faith, rather than following an unquestioned external dogma of the past:

To survive,
Let the past
Teach you—
Past customs,
Struggles,
Leaders and thinkers.
Let

These
Help you.
Let them inspire you,
Warn you,
Give you strength.
But beware:
God is change.
Past is past.
What was Cannot
Come again.
To survive,
Know the past.
Let it touch you.
Then let
The past
Go. (373–374)

This excerpt, which precedes chapter 21, recognizes the influences of the past while facilitating a withdrawal from what no longer functions in the post-apocalyptic diegetic present. In another epigraph, the scriptures align the Earthseed religion with the maternal, but even the new maternal religion must be left in the past if that would further Earthseed's belief in "Destiny": the human colonization of other planets:

Earthseed is adulthood.
It's trying our wings,
Leaving our mother,
Becoming men and women.
We've been children,
Fighting for the full breasts,
The protective embrace,
The soft lap.
Children do this.
But Earthseed is adulthood.
Adulthood is both sweet and sad.
It terrifies.
It empowers.
We are men and women now.
We are Earthseed.
And the Destiny of Earthseed
Is to take root among the stars. (392)

This epigraph points to the inherent empowering nature of the Earthseed religion, which leaves behind the maternal aspects of Earth in order to embody that maternity on other planets, as adults who will facilitate the birth of new communities "among the stars." This enormous transition will require a sort of maturity that human beings have not been compelled to embrace before, which "terrifies," but as an embrace of change, will in effect embrace Earthseed's God.

Both these epigraphs and the rewritten Great Book scaffold new societies that emerge from the detritus of the patriarchal post-apocalyptic society. These women, mothers and daughters, all individually and collectively take up the mantle of reconceiving a new order where the maternal is celebrated and empowering. The new societies in these novels are, in essence, rewritings of the entire genre of the novelistic post-apocalypse.

MATERNAL AFROFUTURISM

The novels discussed in this chapter are written by African American women and are instances of speculative fiction centered on African or African American characters. When examining these novels afrofuturistically, they both perform a countergeneology with regard to African and African diaspora history by imagining a future in which black mothers may write or rewrite the core scriptures that will undergird a post-apocalyptic culture, community, or society. They also re-imagine one of the most grim yet formative events of Afro-diasporic history—the exploitative and violent domination of one ethnic group over another. Both of the novels contribute to a new genre that is "increasingly recognizing the significance of black and postcolonial speculative fiction as discrete genres. . . . This reading of black experience as fundamentally speculative can be applied not only to African Americans, but also to Afro-Caribbeans and other members of the African diaspora, who share similar historical experiences of dislocation, isolation, and alienation" (Burnett, 136). The linkages between both of the novels contribute to a conversation about not only these similar historical experiences, but these experiences through the lens of maternal characters.

The term "Afrofuturism" is typically attributed to Mark Dery, from *South Atlantic Quarterly* in 1993, as

> speculative fiction that treats African American themes and addresses African American concerns in the context of twentieth-century technoculture—and, more generally, African American signification that appropriates images of technology and a prosthetically enhanced future. (736)

The term has broadened since then to include the entirety of speculative fiction emerging from the African diaspora, particularly work that functions counterhistorically. Octavia Butler's oeuvre is considered by literary scholars as paradigmatic of Afrofuturism, and *Parable of the Talents* is an example of maternal Afrofuturism. Butler's work is often cited as a hallmark of black speculative fiction, and Mark Bould states that the

> pantheon of black sf—which included Samuel Delany and Octavia Butler . . . is "a point of cultural departure" for all of these writers . . . because . . . of worst-case futures-of hells-on-Earth and being in them—which are woven into every kind of everyday present reality. . . . The "central fact" of the black sf they produce is an acknowledgement that Apocalypse already happened. (180)

In other words, Butler's novel portrays a post-apocalypse that is a reflection of the present, particularly the present-day experiences of most African American mothers.

In the case of Okorafor's novel, "the novel's speculative metaphor rather directly references the transatlantic slave trade and the centuries of colonialism that followed. In doing so, the book connects Africa's own struggles to those of the African diaspora" (Burnett, 142). This connection occurs in the particular relationship between the Nuru and Okeke, one of which brutalizes, enslaves, and massacres the other. In the case of Butler's novel, her Acorn community is invaded and ravaged by the Christian America Crusaders who, like the Nuru, weaponize rape to keep the women of the community "in line," and enslave all of the Acorn inhabitants and brutally abuse them as they perform forced labor. The idea of the maternal takes on new meaning in these scenes in both novels, where women are forcibly impregnated or whose children are taken away to be enslaved, or are simply murdered. This abusive interchange necessitates heroism on a supernatural scale to bring about transformation, and is carried out by characters whose profound empathy stems from their own experiences of abuse.

Born in Cincinnati to Igbo immigrant parents, the writer Nnedi Okorafor states that Afrofuturism is the *raison d'être* for "the indomitable female protagonists that so often populate magical Nigerian landscapes of her stories" (Whitted, 207). In an interview, Okorafor states, "I see the world as a magical place and therefore that's how it comes out in my work. I am interested in looking into the future, usually that of Africa and that's why what I write is considered Afrofuturism" (Whitted, 208). The inclusiveness of the term has allowed writing such as Okorafor's novel to foster diversity of the genre and to bring attention to work that does not otherwise fit in conventional post-apocalyptic subgenres. This diversity further extends to her portrayals of maternity, which further extend the intersectional inclusivity of Afrofuturism.

Okorafor, in a 2014 interview, distinguishes her Afrofuturist novel from popular white writers' speculative fiction. She states that African speculative fiction

> is not the science fiction equivalent of the black Barbie doll, who is just a white Barbie doll with darker skin. Unlike the traditional Western worldview . . . the African worldview, despite the influence of organized religion . . . still includes the mystical. The mystical and the mundane coexist. And the mystical is not seen as whimsical magic, people *believe* in it. This makes for some very interesting sf, and it requires a different kind of reading from Western audiences. (Langer, 249)

This difference encompasses the mystical maternal as well, as maternity is often portrayed as intertwined with the protagonist's mysticism. Okorafor states, in a separate interview, that "To be African is to merge technology and magic. That's a bold statement to make . . . but so be it. In my experience as an African, the mystical and the mundane have always coexisted" (Whitted, 209).

Okorafor's work has been compared to conventional post-apocalyptic narratives and has been further described as the "Nigerian Harry Potter." Okorafor's response is that

> these comparisons are often a reaction reviewers have to dealing with cultures they find are unfamiliar. By boiling my work down to what is familiar to them, they therefore don't have to discuss those many things that are not familiar to them. (Whitted, 210)

She directs this response not only to the Harry Potter comparison, but also in response to her controversial inclusion of female circumcision in her novel and in other stories. With regard to *this* topic, she states that "they are issues that have been around me nearly all my life. They are real to me. They are not an academic discussion. They are not distant. I know people who have been circumcised" (Whitted, 208). Okorafor's frank and unapologetic inclusion of circumcision, her focus on the uterus, and her candor on other topics that are often profane to Western readers is a means to introduce a challenging unfamiliarity of cultures often unknown in the "conventional" post-apocalyptic genre.

CONCLUSION

These novels illustrate the intersectional possibilities of a new post-apocalyptic society emerging from a post-catastrophe belief system that centers maternal women in their conception. The books' regenerating visions reflect significantly distinct implications for the diverse peoples who engage with these innovative products of the genre. These distinctions are particularly apparent between mothers and daughters in a context of devastated landscapes, where the detritus of the past is everywhere, being remade into technology for the new. The stories are complex, and there are no clear Manichean "good versus evil" divisions in the novels. In Butler's novel, Oya and others clearly endure oppression from patriarchal, fascist, and despotic groups. Yet, Oya's daughter feels that she was neglected and even abandoned by her mother, and assumed that Oya's religion was an unhealthy obsession with a cult following. Onyesonwu's mother was a victim of widespread and weaponized rape at the hands of an ethnic group, the Nuru, who sought to eliminate another ethnic group, the Okeke. However, in order to fight the Nuru, Okeke children were kidnapped and forced into the military, as was the case with the character Mwita. And both ethnic groups condoned the worst aspects of the Great Book, and they perpetuated the patriarchal oppression of women and the maternal. Nevertheless, each of the novel's protagonists, Oya and Onyesonwu, sought to rewrite the stories of their cultures and bring about a new society that lauded the maternal rather than oppressing and weaponizing maternity.

Both writers Butler and Okorafor have, through their novels, *themselves* performed modes of "rewriting" that echo the rewritings of their fictional protagonists. Butler rewrites a biblical parable, one that operates as a cautionary tale for the exploitation of the impoverished and vulnerable, as a revelation of how present-day abuses may one day lead to extremes of fascist leadership and reinstantiation of biblical oppression of women. Okorafor's novel rewrites a tragedy based on a news story from the *Associated Press*, titled "We Want to Make a Light Baby" (2004), which describes an ethnic cleansing campaign taking place in Sudan where Janjaweed Arab militants are attempting to remove and erase African residents. In the Arab culture in Sudan, ethnicity is connected to the father or paternal figure, and the Janjaweed are using systematic rape to "humiliate the women . . . and to weaken tribal ethnic lines. . . . They want more Arab babies to take the land" (Wax). In this news story, over one million non-Arab Africans have been forced from their homes due to the violence that is focused on women through ethnic cleansing and colonization centered on maternity—their potential for impregnation. This is not a new form of eradicating a group of people motivated by theft of resources, as Sarah Deer states:

> Rape and sexual violence are deeply embedded in the colonial mindset. Rape is more than a metaphor for colonization—it is part and parcel of colonization. . . . Sexual assault mimics the worst traits of colonization in its attack on the body, invasion of physical boundaries, and disregard for humanity. . . . The

perpetrators of sexual assault and colonization thrive on power and control over their victims. (150)

Okorafor re-imagines this maternal violence by empowering one of these children resulting from weaponized rape. She re-visions the child's mixed ethnic lineage not as a means of erasure, but as an avenue to right the terrible wrongs inflicted on thousands of women.

By bending the post-apocalyptic novelistic genre toward an affirmation of maternity rather than utilizing motherhood as a trope to illustrate the depravity and abuses of the future, these writers envision a means of empowering women in the present day. These novels provide an aspirational look toward a post-catastrophe that in turn compels their readers to revision the abuses of women today with regard to maternity and the exploitation of women's fertility or potential fertility. These authors revision maternity as emancipatory, not as a debilitating condition or a means of exploiting women's bodies, a sign of moral depravity, or even a duty. This re-visioning requires a cultural shift with regard to mothers and the maternal, and these novels ask us to consider the question, what would our society, writ large, look like if maternity was seen as heroic?

Conclusion

Material Memory: Maternity in the Future Present

The novels examined in this monograph will not be the last to address the amniotic space as the maternal fulcrum of the uncertain survival of humankind in the post-apocalypse. The interest in narratives of the maternal apocalypse is a growing one, reflecting the demand in all forms of media culture to reimagine maternity. Maternity is so often a process and period that has been historically shunned or remained hidden, and its esoteric treatment has led to an absence of the maternal from possibilities of heroism and agency in literary fiction such as the post-apocalypse. The demand for the dismissal of this aversion is apparent in the burgeoning maternal post-apocalypse genre. The concern for maternal care in the non-diegetic present day is one demanding attention from political figures, and though there is yet little interest in placing maternal care at the forefront of a capitalist society, the demand is great.

With the emergence of the post-apocalyptic genre in the nineteenth century, the possibility for an intrepid maternity rarely entered the narrative. Most literary scholars agree that Mary Shelley's *The Last Man* (1826) is the first published post-apocalyptic novel. Although maternal characters do appear in the novel, they die off as a result of the novel's apocalyptic plague. The post–World War II rise in popularity of post-apocalyptic novels only reaffirmed the narrative submission of maternity, and the subsequent inclusion of heroic characters extended to persons of color, spectrums of class, and women, but almost never featured maternal characters. Well-known novels such as *Brave New World* (1931); *Nineteen Eighty-Four* (1949); and the young-adult novel, *The Giver* (1993) are highly lauded novels that all address the question of fertility and reproduction. However, these narratives are centered on the various means of exerting control over—and sometimes conducting the elimination of— women's potential for pregnancy. Population growth is restricted in some case, and the novels emphasize the obsolescence of maternity rather than its possibilities as a force to fight back and exert agency within a world in collapse. It is fascinating that the primary means by which a decimated population may survive and grow again is through valorization of maternity, but it is precisely this process that is elided from post-apocalyptic novels.

What are the implications, then, of the reemergence of the maternal? The novels analyzed in this monograph demonstrate a new awakening to the possibilities of maternity today, pointing to the ways in which the increasing conspicuousness of maternity touches on more concrete societal fears. As noted in this monograph's introduction, the populations of developed nations are declining, and with the devastation of the COVID-19 pandemic, there is an increased awareness of the precarity of life and, possibly, the precarity of healthy maternity. Experiences of population decline further bring issues of maternal sovereignty and freedom of choice to wider attention, and the fear of the loss of sovereignty may very likely feed into the growing popularity and publication of maternal post-apocalypse novels.

Despite continued inequity, women are becoming far more highly educated and are increasingly reaching for scholarly, technological, scientific, and other career goals equal to or beyond men that are unprecedented in modern history. Unfortunately, too often the societies that do not hinder women from the pursuit of higher education and career goals simultaneously compel them to choose a career *or* children, but not both. With little support for maternity in a capitalistic society, women are increasingly choosing to forgo the possibility of maternal aspirations in pursuit of career goals. The solution is, of course, not to inhibit women from pursuing career achievements, but in changing social values to support women who seek a career and a life that includes maternity.

Yet, these improving developments in women's education and career fall apart when threatened by apocalyptic events. To use the COVID-19 pandemic as a case study, numerous reports and news articles published alarming statistics with regard to women stepping away from their careers in order to care for children during the general economic shutdown caused by the quarantine. For example, the Center for American Progress published an article titled "How COVID-19 Sent Women's Workforce Progress Backward," citing harrowing statistic of the fact that four times as many women as men were compelled to quit their jobs due to the collapse in childcare, stating that

> mothers will continue to shoulder the majority of family caregiving and responsibilities, as they have both historically and thus far in the pandemic. Mothers of color will be the most affected. This will have a significant negative effect on women's employment and labor force participation rates. (Kashen)

This maternal collapse points to the fear that may motivate the publication and popularity of novels of the maternal post-apocalypse. Alongside the many accomplishments women have achieved in sovereignty over their bodies and livelihoods in developed nations, this autonomy has always been under threat when built on a shaky foundation that does not form solid structures for caregiving and support for children. Imagining a suffering world that promotes maternity and maternal support instead of disregarding it is a logical imaginative outlet.

As this monograph has demonstrated, bending the post-apocalyptic novelistic genre toward an affirmation of maternity rather than utilizing motherhood as a trope to illustrate the depravity and abuses of the future has brought about the potential to envision a means of empowering women in the present day. These novels illustrate an aspirational regard toward a post-catastrophe that in turn compels their readers to re-vision the inequities and oppressions of maternity and the exploitation of women's fertility or potential fertility. These authors reimagine maternity as emancipatory—not incapacitating, an opportunity for exploitation of maternity, or as a moral judgment. This re-visioning requires a cultural shift with regard to mothers and the maternal, and in imagining this shift, these novels ask us to consider: how would our society, writ large, transform if maternity was perceived as heroic?

Afterword

At the time of final editing for this monograph, the prestigious Nebula Award winners for the year 2021 were announced. One of the winners, a short story, is titled "Badass Moms in the Zombie Apocalypse," by Rae Carson. The story centers on a woman, Brit, who must stay one step ahead of a zombie horde as she is in labor, stopping with each contraction as the zombies close in on her and her lover, Marisol. The zombies have discovered them precisely because the protagonist has gone into labor: "The undead are like sharks, drawn to blood, but they're drawn to birth even more." As they pass by the members of their enclave in their escape, Brit is called a "selfish bitch" as she hurries past because of the fact that she allowed herself to get and stay pregnant. The story describes a woman having to kill her own daughter because she was infected by the undead:

> When Eileen found her, she had to drive her own dagger into her daughter's brain. I put my hand to my giant belly. Is it horrible to bring a person into the world, knowing you might have to send them right back out of it before they've hardly lived? Maybe that's what Liz meant when she called me selfish.

> In a zombie apocalypse, the undead

function as figures against which we can consider our own humanity. After all, zombies shamble upon the metaphorical boundary between human and inhuman. They are a "blank template" onto which we graft all sorts of human anxieties. . . . Because they were once human, they simultaneously serve as a threat of what we might become and a mirror for what we are. (Cohen and Pielak, 44)

The fact that the protagonists of this story are considered selfish for daring to procreate, and are punished for it by attracting the attention of the undead horde that is able to seek out the maternal in particular, points to numerous contemporary anxieties with regard to maternity. In the United States, childbirth rates have declined by about 2 percent each year since 2014, dropping to 4 percent since the COVID-19 pandemic. Reasons for this include rises in unemployment and the decreasing availability of housing and food. Stories such as Carson's, and its reception of prestigious awards, point to growing attention to an undercurrent of anxiety that seems to be embodied by fictional apocalyptic events. The COVID-19 pandemic/apocalypse starkly revealed the inequity and inequalities in our society, worldwide but especially in the United States. Maternal ambitions seem to be increasingly seen as either pipe dreams or afflictions to be avoided, and the increasing frenzy to restrict women's right to abortions is being met by increasing activism to safeguard women's autonomy. We see the metaphorical zombie roaming amid our present context, and its threat to maternity is the most ignored—but arguably the direst—consequence of the contemporary post-apocalypse.

In Carson's tale, Brit and her family are rescued by women who lure away the undead with "menstrual lures," and insist that they risked their lives voluntarily: "Our bodies, our choice" one woman declares. The burgeoning genre of the maternal post-apocalypse points to a threatened future that is saved by placing maternity and the possibilities of maternal choice at the forefront of social concern, and by valorizing all physiological maternal processes rather than demeaning them. Perhaps this growing body of fiction can equip us for a world in which we can all thrive by transforming our assumptions of the maternal.

Works Cited

Anatol, Giselle Liza. "A Feminist Reading of Soucouyants in Nalo Hopkinson's *Brown Girl in the Ring* and *Skin Folk*." *Mosaic: An Interdisciplinary Critical Journal*, vol. 37, no. 3, 2004, pp. 33–50.
Anatol, Giselle Liza. "Maternal Discourses in Nalo Hopkinson's *Midnight Robber*." *African American Review*, vol. 40, no. 1, Spring, 2006, pp. 111–124.
Anderson, Reynaldo. "Afrofuturism 2.0 & the Black Speculative Arts Movement: Notes on a Manifesto." *Obsidian*, vol. 42, no. 1/2, 2016, pp. 228–236.
Atwood, Margaret. *Maddaddam*. Anchor Books, 2013.
Atwood, Margaret. *The Handmaid's Tale*. Anchor Books, 1998.
Beardsley, James. "On the Transcendent in Landscapes of Contemplation." *Contemporary Landscapes of Contemplation*. Ed. Rebecca Krinke. New York: Routledge, 2005.
Beauvoir, Simone. *The Second Sex*. Vintage, 2011.
Beckett, Katherine. "Feminism and the Politics of Childbirth in the United States." *Feminist Theory*, vol. 6, no. 3, 2005, pp. 251–275.
Bhabha, Homi K. *The Location of Culture*. Routledge, 1994.
Biale, David. "The End of Enlightenment?" *Jewish Social Studies*, vol. 22, no. 3, 2017, pp. 141–145.
Bishop, Kyle William. *American Zombie Gothic: The Rise and Fall (and Rise) of the Walking Dead in Popular Culture*. Jefferson, NC; London. McFarland & Company, Inc., Publishers. 2010.
Bould, Mark. "The Ships Landed Long Ago: Afrofuturism and Black SF." *Science Fiction Studies*, vol. 34, no. 2, Afrofuturism 2007, pp. 177–186.
Brettler, M., C. Newsom, and P. Perkins (Eds.). *The New Oxford Annotated Bible with Apocrypha*, 4th ed. Oxford University Press, 2016.
Brin, David. *The Postman*. Spectra. 1997.
Bryce, Jane. "African Futurism: Speculative Fictions and 'Rewriting the Great Book'." *Research in African Literatures*, vol. 50, no. 1, 2019, pp. 1–19.

Burnett, Joshua Yu. "The Great Change and the Great Book: Nnedi Okorafor's Postcolonial, Post-Apocalyptic Africa and the Promise of Black Speculative Fiction." *Research in African Literatures*, vol. 46, no. 4, 2015.

Bustamonte, Elena Clemente. "Fragments and Crossroads in Nalo Hopkinson's Brown Girl in the Ring." *Spaces of Utopia: An Electronic Journal*, no. 4, 2007, pp. 11–30.

Butler, Judith. *Gender Trouble: Feminism and the Subversion of Identity*. New York: Routledge, 1999.

Butler, Judith. "The Body Politics of Julia Kristeva." *Hypatia*. vol. 3, no. 3, 1989, pp. 104–118.

Butler, Octavia. *Parable of the Talents*. Grand Central Publishing, 2019.

Carson, Rae. "Badass Moms in the Zombie Apocalypse." *Uncanny: A Magazine of Science Fiction and Fantasy*, no. 32, 2020.

Carter, Shannon K. "Gender and Childbearing Experiences: Revisiting O'Brien's Dialectics of Reproduction." *NWSA Journal*, vol. 21, no. 2, 2009, pp. 121–143.

Chavkin, Nancy Feyl and Allen Chavkin. *Conversations with Louise Edrich and Michael Dorris*. Jackson, MS: University of Mississippi, 1994.

Checker, Melissa. *Polluted Promises: Environmental Racism and the Search for Justice in a Southern Town*. NYU Press, 2005.

Chau, Adam Yuet. "The Nation in Religion and Religion in the Nation." *Religion and Nationalism in Chinese Societies*. Ed. Cheng-tian Kuo. Amsterdam: Amsterdam UP, 2017.

Cohen, Alexander and Chase Pielak. "Yes, but in a Zombie Apocalypse . . ." *Modern Language Studies*, vol. 43, no. 2, 2014, pp. 44–57.

Coleman, Monica A. "Serving the Spirits: The Pan-Caribbean African-Derived Religion in Nalo Hopkinson's *Brown Girl in the Ring*." *Journal of Caribbean Literatures*, vol. 6, no. 1, 2009, pp. 1–13.

Collins, Patricia Hill and Sirma Bilge. *Intersectionality*. Malden: Polity Press, 2018.

De Sherbinin, Julie W. *Chekhov and Russian Religious Culture: The Poetics of the Marian Paradigm*. Evanston: Northwestern UP, 1997.

Deer, Sarah. "Decolonizing Rape Law: A Native Feminist Synthesis of Safety and Sovereignty." *Wicazo Sa Review*, vol. 24, no. 2, 2009, pp. 149–167.

Delgado, Richard. *Critical Race Theory: An Introduction*. NYU Press, 2017.

Delgado, Richard and Jean Stefancic. *Critical Race Theory: An Introduction*. New York UP, 2017.

Derrida, Jacques. *Archive Fever*. University of Chicago P, 2017.

———. "No Apocalypse, Not Now (Full Speed Ahead, Seven Missiles, Seven Missives)." *Diacritics*, vol. 14, no. 2, 1984, pp. 20–31.

Dery, Mark. "Black to the Future." *South Atlantic Quarterly,* vol. 92, no. 4, 1993, pp. 735–778.

Drezner, Daniel. "Metaphor of the Living Dead: Or, the Effect of the Zombie Apocalypse on Public Policy Discourse." *Social Research*, vol. 81, no. 4, 2014, pp. 825–849.

Duncan, Carol B. "Hard Labour: Religion, Sexuality and the Pregnant Body in the African Diaspora." *Journal of the Association for Research on Mothering*, vol. 7, no. 1 (2005), pp. 167–173.

Elison, Meg. *The Book of the Unnamed Midwife*. New York: 47North, 2016.
Erdrich, Louise. *Future Home of the Living God*. New York: Harper, 2017.
Fifer, Elizabeth. "Dead Reckoning: The Darkening Landscape of Contemporary World Literature." *World Literature Today* (March/April 2017), pp. 43–48.
Gilbert, Sandra M. and Susan Gubar. *The Madwoman in the Attic*. New Haven: Yale UP, 2000.
Gingrey, John Phillip. "Maternal Mortality: A US Public Health Crisis." *American Journal of Public Health*, vol. 110, no. 4, 2020, pp. 462–464.
Gutjahr, Paul. "Sacred Texts in the United States." *Book History*, 2001, vol. 4, 2001, pp. 335–370.
Hermann, Heinrich. "On the Transcendent in Landscapes of Contemplation." *Contemporary landscapes of contemplation*. Ed. R. Krinke. London: Routledge, 2005, pp. 36–72.
Hirsch, Marianne. *The Mother/Daughter Plot: Narrative, Psychoanalysis, Feminism*. Bloomington: Indiana UP, 1989.
Hopkinson, Nalo. *Brown Girl in the Ring*. Hachette Book Group, 2012.
Hoving, Isabel. *In Praise of New Travelers: Reading Caribbean Migrant Women's Writing*. Stanford, CA: Stanford UP, 2001.
Hutton, Ronald. *The Witch: A History of Fear, from Ancient Times to the Present*. New Haven: Yale UP, 2017.
Iman Jackson, Zakiyyah. *Becoming Human: Matter and Meaning in an Antiblack World*. New York: New York UP, 2020.
James, P.D. *Children of Men*. Vintage Books, 1996.
Jacobs, Amber. *On Matricide: Myth, Psychoanalysis, and the Law of the Mother*. New York: Columbia UP, 2007.
Kashen, Julie. "How COVID-19 Sent Women's Workforce Progress Backward." Center for American Progress, October 2020.
Kristeva, Julia and Arthur Goldhammer. "Stabat Mater." *Poetics Today*, vol. 6, no. 1/2, *The Female Body in Western Culture: Semiotic Perspectives* (1985), pp. 133–152.
Lauretis, Teresa de. *Alice Doesn't: Feminism, Semiotics, Cinema*. Indiana UP, 1984.
Lisboa, Maria Manuel. *The End of the World: Apocalypse and Its Aftermath in Western Culture*. Open Book Publishers, 2011.
Luttwak, Edward N. *Coup d'État: A Practical Handbook*. Harvard UP, 2016.
Martínez-Falquina, Silvia. "My Body Not My Own: An Intersectional View on Relationality in Fiction by Toni Morrison and Louise Erdrich." *Lectora: Revista de dona i textualitat*. vol. 26, 2020. pp. 117–132.
Martínez-Falquina, Silvia. "Louise Erdrich's Future Home of the Living God: Uncertainty, Proleptic Mourning and Relationality in Native Dystopia." *Atlantis*, vol. 41 no. 2, 2019, pp. 161–178.
McBean, Sam. "Feminism and Futurity: Revisiting Marge Piercy's *Woman on the Edge of Time*." *Feminist Review*, no. 107, 2014, pp. 37–56.
McCarthy, Cormac. *The Road*. New York: Vintage Books, 2006.
Mignolo, Walter. "Epistemic Disobedience, Independent Thought, and De-colonial Freedom." *Theory, Culture & Society*, vol. 26, no. 7–8, 2009, pp. 1–23.

Moynagh, Maureen. "Speculative Pasts and Afro-Futures: Nalo Hopkinson's Trans-American Imaginary." *African American Review*, vol. 51, no. 3, 2018, pp. 211–222.

Murphy, Graham J. "Considering Her Ways: In(ter)secting Matriarchal Utopias." *Science Fiction Studies*, vol. 35, no. 2, 2008, pp. 266–280.

Nash, Jennifer. "The Political Life of Black Motherhood." *Feminist Studies* vol. 44, no. 3, 2018, pp. 699–712.

New American Standard Bible. La Habra, CA: Foundation Publications, for the Lockman Foundation, 1971.

Nkenana, Akhona. "No African Futures without the Liberation of Women: A Decolonial Feminist Perspective." *Africa Development / Afrique et Développement: Transforming Global Relations for a Just World/Transformer les relations internationales pour un monde juste*, vol. 40, no. 3, 2015, pp. 41–57.

O'Brien, Mary. *The Politics of Reproduction*. Routledge & Kegan Paul. 1981.

Ojaide, Tanure. "Modern African Literature and Cultural Identity." *African Studies Review*, vol. 35, no. 3, 1992, pp. 43–57.

Okorafor, Nnedi. *Who Fears Death*. New York: DAW, 2011.

Pechilis, Karen. "Illuminating Women's Religious Authority through Ethnography." *Journal of Feminist Studies in Religion*, vol. 29, no. 1, 2013, pp. 93–101.

Piercy, Marge. *Woman on the Edge of Time*. New York: Ballantine Books, 1997.

Reid, E. Shelley. "The Stories We Tell: Louise Erdrich's Identity Narratives." *MELUS*, vol. 25, no. 3/4, 2000, pp. 65–86.

Rich, Adrienne. *Of Woman Born*. New York: W.W. Norton & Company, 1995.

Rogan, Alcena Madeline Davis. "Tananarive Due and Nalo Hopkinson Revisit the Reproduction of Mothering Legacies of the Past and Strategies for the Future." *Afro-Future Females: Black Writers Chart Science Fiction's Newest New-Wave Trajectory*. Ed. Marleen S. Barr Columbus: Ohio State University Press, 2008, pp. 75–99.

Roshanravan, Shireen. "Motivating Coalition: Women of Color and Epistemic Disobedience." *Hypatia*, vol. 29, no. 1, 2014, pp. 41–58.

Rothman, Barbara Katz. "Beyond Mothers and Fathers: Ideology in a Patriarchal Society." *Mothering: Ideology, Experience, and Agency*. Ed. Evelyn Nakano Glenn, Grace Chang, Linda Rennie Forcey. New York: Routledge, 1994.

Ruffin, Kimberly. "Parable of a 21st Century Religion: Octavia Butler's Afrofuturistic Bridge between Science and Religion." *Obsidian III*, vol. 6, no. 2, 20006, pp. 87–104.

Shelley, Mary Wollstonecraft. *The Last Man*. Wordsworth Editions, Ltd, 2004.

Stover, E. D. and Eric W. Mercure. "The Pomegranate: A New Look at the Fruit of Paradise." *HortScience*, vol. 2, no. 5, 2007, pp. 1088–1092.

Tegethoff, Marion, et al. "Maternal Psychosocial Stress during Pregnancy and Placenta Weight: Evidence from a National Cohort Study." *PLoS One*, vol. 5, no. 12, 2011.

Thornton, Megan. "Epigraphs, Intertextuality, and Exile: Reading the Poetry of Zoé Valdés." *Letras Femeninas*, vol. 39, no. 2, 2013, pp. 151–165.

Tiffin, Helen. "Cold Hearts and (Foreign) Tongues: Recitation and the Reclamation of the Female Body in the Works of Erna Brodber and Jamaica Kincaid." *Callaloo*, vol. 16, no. 4, 1993, pp. 909–921.

Tourino, Christina. "Ethnic Reproduction and the Amniotic Deep: Joy Kogawa's 'Obasan'." *Frontiers: A Journal of Women Studies*, vol. 24, no. 1, 2003, pp. 134–153.

Walker, Michelle Boulous. *Philosophy and the Maternal Body: Reading Silence*. London: Routledge, 1998.

Warner-Lewis, Maureen. "The Oral Tradition in the African Diaspora." *The Cambridge History of African and Caribbean Literature*. New York: Cambridge UP, 2004.

Watkins, Susan. "Future Shock: Rewriting the Apocalypse in Contemporary Women's Fiction." *Lit: Literature Interpretation Theory*, vol. 23, no. 2, 2012, 119–137.

Wax, Emily. "We Want to Make a Light Baby." Washington Post, June 30, 2004.

Whitted, Qiana. "To Be African is to Merge Magic and Technology." *Afrofuturism 2.0: The Rise of Astro-Blackness*. Ed Reynaldo Anderson, Charles E. Jones. New York: Lexington Books, 2016.

Žižek, Slavoj. *Pandemic! 2: Chronicles of a Time Lost*. New York: OR Books, 2020.

Index

ambivalence, 11, 46, 59, 60, 73
anxiety, 2, 13, 37, 64, 84, 93, 98, 102, 139, 140
apathy, 2
apokalypsis, 6
autocracy/autocratic, 7, 20, 31, 36, 37, 40
autonomy, 6, 7, 10, 11, 13, 15, 18, 22, 24, 31, 40, 48, 51, 58, 63, 67, 68, 79, 137, 140

barbarism, 6
birth rates, 1, 139
Butler, Judith, 5, 9–11, 42, 45, 46, 67, 68, 81, 87, 88, 98, 105

chiasmus, 8
civilization, 2, 3, 6, 7, 34, 43, 44, 94, 102, 121, 125
climate change. *See* extreme weather events
COVID-19, 1, 11, 32, 136, 140

death drive, 64, 65
democracy/democratic, 31, 80
displacement, 2, 27
domination, 5, 23, 30, 51, 52, 63, 71, 89, 131
dystopia/dystopian, 2, 6, 7, 22, 31, 77, 80, 99, 101, 106, 108, 109, 128

enslavement. *See* slavery
eschatology, 58
exoticism, 25, 30
exploitation, 3, 9, 22, 26, 27, 47, 50, 53, 70, 95, 97, 101–3, 112, 118, 134, 137
extinction, 3, 15, 18, 35, 42, 65, 66
extreme weather events, 1

feminism, 5, 8, 14, 22, 23, 50
fertility, 4, 5
forced pregnancy, 5, 10, 23, 27, 47, 63, 68, 115, 124, 132, 134
Freud, 14, 15, 64, 65

gravida, 7, 13–19, 21–24, 34–36, 38, 40, 77, 124

heterosexual/heteronormative, 30, 45, 68, 71, 74

identity, 8, 11, 16, 25–27, 30, 38, 42–46, 59, 60, 63, 94, 111, 117, 120
intersectionality, 6, 8, 22, 44, 79, 80, 132, 133

journal, 38, 42, 43, 46, 66, 73–75
journey, 14, 20, 44, 45, 54, 58, 67

kidnap, 8, 9, 21, 22, 29, 30, 51, 52, 109, 114, 116, 121, 133
Kristeva, Julia, 11, 48–50, 55

leadership, 4, 7, 22, 55, 108, 121, 134

maternal mortality, 1, 9, 89, 124
maternal post-apocalypse, 6, 7, 10, 11, 22, 49, 51, 135, 136, 140
maternal turn, 6, 19, 41, 68
matriarchal, 72, 73
monster, 15, 60, 63, 95

natal (pre and postnatal), 6, 8, 9, 61
nationalism, 34, 35

obeah, 79, 82, 85, 88, 92, 93, 95, 96, 98, 99, 101, 102, 104
orisha, 78, 92, 93, 99, 101

patriarchy/patriarchal, 2, 5, 7–11, 14, 15, 20, 22, 31, 41, 42, 44, 46, 47, 49, 50, 54, 56, 58–60, 62–64, 67–72, 74, 75, 81, 86–90, 92, 96–101, 104, 108–12, 114–16, 118, 123–25, 130, 133
pregnancy. *See* gravida

quiescence, 8, 51, 71, 122

racism/racist, 9, 35, 78, 80, 85, 86, 113, 116
rebirth, 3, 64, 98, 127. *See also* renaissance
regenerative/regeneration, 3–5, 7, 11, 16, 20, 38, 47, 67, 126, 133

religion, 8, 29, 78, 86, 89, 92, 98, 107, 108, 110–17, 119, 122, 128–30, 132–34
renaissance, 3, 93
reproductive coercion. *See* forced pregnancy

Shelley, Mary, 60, 135
silencing, 48, 52, 101
slavery, 2, 5, 7, 13, 21, 27, 43–45, 47–53, 56, 61, 69, 74, 79, 86, 87, 92, 100, 104, 111, 114, 115, 125, 132
speculative, 2, 6, 9, 13, 31, 51, 78, 131, 132
state-sponsored abuse, 3, 5, 47
stillbirth, 7, 43, 66, 67, 73, 74
suicide, 5, 51, 55, 68, 87
symbolic, 9–11, 42–44, 46, 49, 50, 54–56, 58, 60–62, 64, 65, 69, 71–73, 80, 81, 84, 87–89, 98, 109

trouble, 5, 9–11, 42, 45, 67, 68, 79, 100, 101

unnatural, 7, 50, 63, 89, 98, 100, 101
uterus, 5, 6, 8, 20, 32, 47, 118, 119, 133
utopia, 3, 4, 27, 31, 70, 73

violence, 11, 47, 52, 53, 70, 80, 87, 107, 113, 114, 122, 134

wild men, 5, 49

xenophobia, 114, 125

Yoruba, 78, 92, 94, 97

zombies, 2, 139, 140

About the Author

Renae L. Mitchell, PhD, has taught literature and English at the University of New Mexico where she was a faculty member in Los Alamos since 2013. Renae completed her doctorate at Pennsylvania State University in Comparative Literature. In addition to her interest in speculative fiction, Renae has published on the topics of Mexican film studies and on the poet Derek Walcott.

www.ingramcontent.com/pod-product-compliance
Lightning Source LLC
Chambersburg PA
CBHW020125010526
44115CB00008B/975